Rediscovering Rubén Darío through Translation

Rediscovering Rubén Darío through Translation

Carlos F. Grigsby

BLOOMSBURY ACADEMIC
NEW YORK • LONDON • OXFORD • NEW DELHI • SYDNEY

BLOOMSBURY ACADEMIC
Bloomsbury Publishing Inc, 1359 Broadway, New York, NY 10018, USA
Bloomsbury Publishing Plc, 50 Bedford Square, London, WC1B 3DP, UK
Bloomsbury Publishing Ireland, 29 Earlsfort Terrace, Dublin 2, D02 AY28, Ireland

BLOOMSBURY, BLOOMSBURY ACADEMIC and the Diana logo
are trademarks of Bloomsbury Publishing Plc

First published in the United States of America 2024
Paperback edition published 2026

Copyright © Carlos F. Grigsby, 2024

Cover design: Eleanor Rose
Cover photo: Ruben Dario (1912) © Eraza Collection / Alamy

All rights reserved. No part of this publication may be: i) reproduced or transmitted in any form, electronic or mechanical, including photocopying, recording or by means of any information storage or retrieval system without prior permission in writing from the publishers; or ii) used or reproduced in any way for the training, development or operation of artificial intelligence (AI) technologies, including generative AI technologies. The rights holders expressly reserve this publication from the text and data mining exception as per Article 4(3) of the Digital Single Market Directive (EU) 2019/790.

Bloomsbury Publishing Inc does not have any control over, or responsibility for, any third-party websites referred to or in this book. All internet addresses given in this book were correct at the time of going to press. The author and publisher regret any inconvenience caused if addresses have changed or sites have ceased to exist, but can accept no responsibility for any such changes.

Library of Congress Cataloging-in-Publication Data
Names: Grigsby, Carlos F., author.
Title: Rediscovering Rubén Darío through translation / Carlos F. Grigsby.
Description: New York : Bloomsbury Academic, 2024. | Includes bibliographical references and index.
Identifiers: LCCN 2023053802 (print) | LCCN 2023053803 (ebook) | ISBN 9798765119112 (hardback) | ISBN 9798765119129 (paperback) | ISBN 9798765119136 (ebook) | ISBN 9798765119143 (pdf)
Subjects: LCSH: Darío, Rubén, 1867–1916–Criticism and interpretation. | Darío, Rubén, 1867–1916–Translations into English–History and criticism. | LCGFT: Literary criticism.
Classification: LCC PQ7519.D3 Z33166 2024 (print) | LCC PQ7519.D3 (ebook) | DDC 861/.5–dc23/eng/20240130
LC record available at https://lccn.loc.gov/2023053802
LC ebook record available at https://lccn.loc.gov/2023053803

ISBN:	HB:	979-8-7651-1911-2
	PB:	979-8-7651-1912-9
	ePDF:	979-8-7651-1914-3
	eBook:	979-8-7651-1913-6

Typeset by Integra Software Services Pvt. Ltd.

For product safety related questions contact productsafety@bloomsbury.com.

To find out more about our authors and books visit www.bloomsbury.com
and sign up for our newsletters.

To my parents

Contents

Acknowledgments	viii
Introduction	1

Part One Translation in Darío

1 Thinking in French and Writing in Spanish	21
2 Not Only from the Roses of Paris	47

Part Two Darío in Translation

3 English Translations of Rubén Darío	71
Coda: Translating Darío's Poetics of *(H)armonía*	125
Conclusion	135
Notes	138
Bibliography	159
Index	171

Acknowledgments

I would like to thank María del Pilar Blanco and Ben Bollig, for helping me to become a better reader. Many thanks also to Laura Lonsdale for her generous feedback.

Introduction

Ningún problema tan consustancial con las letras y con su modesto misterio como el que propone una traducción.

Discusión, Jorge Luis Borges

Rubén Darío (1867–1916) is a classic of Hispanic literature. As critic Pedro Henríquez Ureña puts it: "Of any poem written in Spanish it can be told with certainty whether it was written before or after him."[1] At the end of the nineteenth century, Rubén Darío shook the Spanish language out of its slumber and put it back in conversation with the literatures of the west. He broke ground for metrical experimentation, opening the way for free verse and spearheading *Modernismo*, the movement which inaugurated modern Spanish American literature. It's a well-known story from Hispanic literary history.

And yet, the Nicaraguan poet is scarcely known in the English-speaking world. According to *The Oxford Guide to Literature in English Translation*, "Interest in Latin American poetry emerged in the 1960s. Before that decade, readership was limited and highly specialized."[2] In the same book, after reading that Neruda, Vallejo, and Paz went on to be translated in the 1970s, we are told the following:

> However, several of the best-known Latin American poets have failed to find English translators of much worth. Besides Gabriela Mistral, the great modernist poets like Rubén Dario and José Martí, the surrealist Vicente Huidobro, the Cuban rhythm poet Nicolás Guillén, or the Christian Marxist Ernesto Cardenal remain relatively unknown in English, despite the occasional attempt at translating some of their works by gifted, enthusiastic translators working with small presses.[3]

Tom Boll's analysis of Penguin's Latin American translations in the 1950s, 1960s, and 1970s confirms this: "With Paz, Penguin completed a list of canonical twentieth-century poets that included Jiménez, Machado, Lorca, Neruda, and Vallejo."[4] There is no mention of Darío, even though those writers who were translated and published by Penguin often recognized his influence on their writing.

Let's start with Peruvian poet César Vallejo. In the following passage, Vallejo is rejecting the generation of *posmodernista* writers that precedes him; in doing so, he rescues *la gran voz inmortal* of one poet:

> De la generación que nos precede no tenemos nada que esperar. Ella es un fracaso para nosotros y para todos los tiempos. Si nuestra generación logra abrirse un camino, su obra aplastará a la anterior. Entonces, la historia de la literatura española saltará sobre los últimos treinta años, como por un abismo Rubén Darío elevará su gran voz inmortal sobre la orilla opuesta y de esta otra, la juventud sabrá qué responder.[5]

When Chilean poet Pablo Neruda and Spanish writer Federico García Lorca were fêted in 1933 at the PEN Club in Buenos Aires, both performed a speech in honor of Darío called "Discurso al alimón," which ended with these words:

> Neruda: Federico García Lorca, español, y yo, chileno, declinamos la responsabilidad de esta noche de camaradas, hacia esa gran sombra que cantó más altamente que nosotros, y saludó con voz inusitada a la tierra argentina que pisamos.
>
> Lorca: Pablo Neruda, chileno, y yo, español, coincidimos en el idioma y en el gran poeta, nicaragüense, argentino, chileno y español, Rubén Darío.
>
> N. & L.: Por cuyo homenaje y gloria levantamos nuestro vaso.[6]

Finally, here is Borges summing up Darío's contribution to literature in Spanish:

> Todo lo renovó Darío: la materia, el vocabulario, la métrica, la magia peculiar de ciertas palabras, la sensibilidad del poeta y de sus lectores. Su labor no ha cesado y no cesará; quienes alguna vez lo combatimos, comprendemos hoy que lo continuamos. Lo podemos llamar El Libertador.[7]

Another way of measuring Darío's influence is by numbers. Tomás Navarro Tomás pointed out that Darío's oeuvre displays thirty-seven different metrical lines and 136 different stanza forms.[8] As Alberto Acereda and Will Derusha remind us, the sheer number of scholarly works inspired by Darío's work is daunting:[9] "Since his death, the volume of works devoted to him is probably greater than that given to any other writer in the history of Spanish and Spanish American literature, with the exception of Cervantes."[10] Why, then, is a poet whose work is inescapable in a major global language almost completely ignored in another, even after being translated several times?

This is one of the questions to which this book provides an answer. Throughout its pages I read Darío's writing through translation. That means looking at not only the place of Darío in the translation of Spanish American literature into English, but also the place of translation in Darío's own writing. The book is therefore made up of two sections. The result is a double-sided painting, as it were: the recto is titled "Translation in Darío" and the verso "Darío in Translation." As I explain in detail, this approach sheds new light on his work: I argue that Darío's poetry is multilingual, an aspect of his writing which has been overlooked.

Due to the sheer scope of Darío scholarship, before explaining my approach I will first consider the evolution of Darío studies over the years to elucidate the place of this book within the corpus.

Rubén Darío Studies, Past and Present

As suggested above, a comprehensive survey of the scholarship published on Darío would demand a monograph of its own.[11] It would also have to cover the various studies on *Modernismo* with a postcolonial, world-literary, or comparative focus which have recently emerged as part of a larger, transnational methodological shift.[12] What I offer here is a necessarily broad picture. My aim is to show how the scholarship on Darío's writing has evolved over the years, so that the place of this book within that corpus can be better understood.

By his own hand, Darío himself largely influenced the reception of his work.[13] As one of the first professional Spanish American writers to problematize the place of literature in modern society—and as one who was cognizant of his own place in history—Darío deliberately shaped *Modernismo*'s reception and remembrance. He was the first to name the movement in a *crónica* from 1890 describing his visit to Peruvian writer Ricardo Palma two years earlier, and in doing so describes it as "un espíritu nuevo que anima a un pequeño pero triunfante y soberbio grupo de escritores y poetas de la América española."[14] He openly called himself the initiator of *Modernismo* in his rejoinder to Franco-Argentine writer Paul Groussac in "Los colores del estandarte" (1896), a claim he would repeat in prefaces and critical writings published afterward, effectively becoming one of the first literary historians of the movement. At other times in his career, as I explore in Chapters 1 and 2, he cast his literary persona as a writer "who thinks in French," before recasting himself, after the Spanish–American war in 1898, as an eminently pan-Hispanic writer.[15] Darío's tales about his life and writings have influenced the hagiographic penchant of his biographers,[16] while his own narrative of *Modernismo* indirectly led to the narrow understanding of the movement as one that essentially began and ended with the Nicaraguan author.[17]

Despite his long shadow, two of his contemporaries greatly impacted the way Darío's writing was read in his lifetime: José Enrique Rodó and Pedro Henríquez Ureña. The former's review of *Prosas profanas* published in 1899 was widely read in its day. It remains an essential text to understand Darío's reception and place in Spanish American literature. While it is a praiseful review overall—to the extent that the author felt compelled to write it in an inspired *modernista* style himself—Rodó seems to have sensed that what Spanish American literary circles of the time wanted to hear was whether Darío was the poet for whom the Americas had been waiting. The Uruguayan essayist cunningly begins his text by stating: "Indudablemente, Rubén Darío no es el poeta de América."[18] The phrase resonates more than the rest of the article, in which Rodó lauds Darío for being an exquisite innovator but faults him for writing poems whose form, though of a marble-like finish, is lacking in outpourings of the heart. Darío would answer Rodó's criticism with the confessional lyricism of some of the best-known poems of *Cantos de vida y esperanza* (1905).

The latter collection was reviewed by Henríquez Ureña, who comments on the previous evolution of Darío's poetry and perceptively grasps the long-lasting influence it would have on Spanish American literature. He would go on to make a valuable contribution to the study of the sources of Darío (discussed in Chapter 2), write the introduction for the first book-length translation of Darío into English (discussed in Chapter 3), and become an important historian of *Modernismo* with his *Literary Currents of Hispanic America,* published in 1945.

After Darío's death in 1916, which seems to have plunged writers from across the Hispanic world into a state of collective mourning, two especially significant contributions to the study of Darío's sources were published: Erwin K. Mapes's *L'influence française dans l'œuvre de Rubén Darío* (1925) and Arturo Marasso's *Rubén Darío y su creación poética* (1934). Mapes's monograph remains the best work on the subject of Darío's relationship to French, whereas Marasso's vast study is the most comprehensive work on the *modernista*'s sources in general. As I will explain, while this book owes much to both monographs, it questions their understanding of the notions of literary influence and imitation, trying to move beyond them in better understanding the sophistication of Darío's engagement with his sources. Mapes went on to edit several hitherto uncollected articles by Darío, published as *Escritos inéditos de Rubén Darío* (1938). In the same decade, Arturo Torres-Rioseco published *Rubén Darío: casticismo y americanismo* (1931), a work which, though limited in its scope, provided ample evidence of Darío's engagement with Spanish and Spanish American sources through his own poetry.[19] Three years later, Raúl Silva Castro published *Obras desconocidas de Rubén Darío* (1934), a large number of uncollected writings by Darío dating from his stay in Chile, thus expanding the understanding of the Nicaraguan poet's time there.

In 1948 Spanish writer Pedro Salinas published one of the essential books of the corpus: *La poesía de Rubén Darío: ensayo sobre el tema y los temas del poeta* (1948). It analyzes Darío's oeuvre as a composite of several subthemes dominated by one overarching theme, which, in Salinas's view, relates to eroticism. While the study offers a sweeping view of Darío's body of poetic work, at times the author seems to subsume texts that require greater nuance and elaboration into the theme of eroticism. If the result is beneficial for the monograph's internal coherence, it comes at the cost of critical nuance and penetration. In the same decade, Diego Manuel Sequeira published *Rubén*

Darío, criollo; o, raíz y médula de su creación poética (1945), a well-researched study that sheds light on Darío's formative years in Central America, detailing his first contact with French literature.

In 1956 Francisca Sánchez, Darío's widow, donated eighty of Darío's folders and nearly 5,000 other documents to the Universidad Complutense of Madrid. This led to the creation of the *Archivo Rubén Darío*, giving rise to several publications, notably a biography of Darío by Antonio Oliver Belmás, *Este otro Rubén Darío* (1960), and hitherto unpublished letters edited by Dietino Álvarez as *Cartas de Rubén Darío: Epistolario inédito del poeta con sus amigos españoles* (1963). The new documents shed light on Darío's relation to Spanish writers and intellectuals, as well as his years spent in Spain. It opened a window onto his private life, which had hitherto remained somewhat elusive given that its portrayal had been usually mediated by Darío himself or his contemporaries.[20] Five years earlier, Nicaraguan poet-scholar Ernesto Mejía Sánchez edited Darío's *Cuentos completos* (1951), in an edition brilliantly prefaced by Raimundo Lida in what remains one of the best studies of Darío's short stories.[21] The edition reasserted the historical value of Darío's treatment of the short story, which helped to introduce the fantastical genre in Argentina, paving the way for authors like Leopoldo Lugones and Jorge Luis Borges. In the same decade, Marasso expanded his tome by publishing a second edition of *Rubén Darío y su creación poética* (1954).

Historically, centennial celebrations seem to spur Darío scholars toward critical breakthroughs in the study of the Nicaraguan author's oeuvre. The decade of the 1960s marked the centenary of the poet's birth. Perhaps as a result, penetrating work was published in those years, in particular Octavio Paz's essay "El caracol y la sirena" (1965), Enrique Anderson Imbert's *La originalidad de Rubén Darío* (1967), and Ángel Rama's *Rubén Darío y el modernismo* (1970). Pedro Luis Barcia edited the first volume of hitherto uncollected articles by Darío, published in 1968 as *Escritos dispersos de Rubén Darío (recogidos de periódicos de Buenos Aires)*, the second volume of which would come out in 1977. Together with Mapes's collection, Barcia's work led the way for Günter Schmigalle's recent editorial work on Darío's journalistic prose, which had been historically ignored despite its immense cultural value for the study of the history and development of Spanish American literature.

Perhaps no two critics have helped more than Paz and Rama in lifting Darío's oeuvre beyond the reach of its detractors and in cementing its canonical status. Alongside Anderson Imbert, their writings offer powerful counterarguments to the notion of the Darío's writing as escapist and affected, opening several critical avenues subsequently explored by critics. Whereas Paz did not publish much else on Darío, Rama thoroughly transformed the way the Nicaraguan poet's work is read thanks to his *El mundo de los sueños* (1973) and *Las máscaras democráticas del modernismo* (1985).

The influence of these authors' work is well known; their names can be found in the bibliography of any work on Darío published since.[22] However, Anderson Imbert's work has not been given the same attention. While it is not innovative in its approach and is less bold in its claims, it's one of the few monographs that cover the entirety of Darío's oeuvre. It offers a comprehensive analysis of the many facets of his writing, such as the intertwinement of his prose and poetry, and includes lucid readings of his journalistic and critical writings. Other important studies published in the years that followed include Françoise Peru's Marxist analysis *Literatura y sociedad en América Latina: el modernismo* (1976), Francisco López Estrada's *Rubén Darío y la edad media* (1971), and Ernesto Mejía Sánchez's *Cuestiones rubendarianas* (1970), alongside the first authoritative edition of Darío's *Poesía* (1970), superbly prefaced by Rama. The poor quality of the editions of Darío's writing is a long-standing issue that reflects the precarious conditions in which Spanish American scholarship has been carried out historically.

The centenary of the publication of *Los raros* and *Prosas profanas* drew near during the 1990s, a decade which saw another wave of important publications on Darío. Among them, it is worth singling out two fresh perspectives on *Modernismo*, both with different focuses: Graciela Montaldo's *La sensibilidad amenazada: tendencias del modernismo latinoamericano* (1995) and Gerard Aching's *The Politics of Spanish American Modernismo: By Exquisite Design* (1997). Both authors look at Darío's work with fresh eyes. The former looks at the shift of cultural values in the Latin American *fin de siècle* from a wider ideological perspective, aiming to encompass the many social and cultural transformations of the epoch. The latter offers insightful analyses of the political dimensions of *Modernismo* and closely reads specific texts by the *modernista*.

In a way, they further Rama's work from the 1970s. In addition, an excellent collection of essays that revaluated the complexity of *Los raros* and *Prosas profanas* was edited by Alfonso García Morales and published as *Rubén Darío: Estudios en el centenario de* Los raros *y* Prosas profanas (1998).

The turn of the century brought Darío scholars closer to the centennial anniversary of the poet's death to be celebrated in 2016, the occasion of which reflected the far-reaching effects of Paz and Rama's investigations mentioned earlier. Darío was now undoubtedly considered a classic of the Spanish language, as is attested by the *Real Academia Española*'s edition of his selected works published by Alfaguara, *Del símbolo a la realidad: Obra selecta. Edición conmemorativa I centenario Rubén Darío* (2016), and the first volume of his complete works published by Galaxia Gutenberg and prepared by Julio Ortega, *Obras completas* (2007). The latter includes one of the most compelling introductions to the Darío's oeuvre to date, an essay by Mexican poet José Emilio Pacheco.

By and large, the increasing digitalization of scholarly output from the 1990s on has increased the frequency at which scholars publish their work—a change which is also reflected in Darío studies. In that respect, a detailed commentary on the publications of the past two decades exceeds the possibilities of these pages. Nevertheless, it's worth singling out Julio Ortega's unorthodox biography of Darío published in 2003: a thought-provoking text that proposes new ways of thinking about the *modernista*'s work. Also, Spanish scholar José María Martínez has made valuable contributions to the study of Darío's sources and collaborations with other poets, as can be read in his *Addenda* (2000) and in recent articles quoted throughout this book. Beatriz Colombi and Susana Zanetti's analysis on Darío's writing for *La Nación*, published in *Rubén Darío en La Nación de Buenos Aires, 1892–1916* (2004), is an invaluable resource thanks to its rigorous documentation and sophisticated analysis of Darío's role as journalist for the Buenos Aires daily. In addition, Günter Schmigalle's unrelenting labor as editor of Darío's prose continues the work begun decades earlier by Mapes, Barcia, and Rama: he has edited new publications of *Los raros* (2015), *La caravana pasa* (2006), and dozens of hitherto uncollected articles published in two volumes as *Crónicas desconocidas* (2006, 2011). He also published a selection of articles on the city of Paris ¿*Va a arder París?: crónicas cosmopolitas, 1892–1912* (2008). More recently, Alejandro Mejías-López's *The Inverted Conquest: The Myth of Modernity and the Transatlantic Onset of Modernism* (2010) sweepingly examines the colonial and racial biases behind notions of modernity as applied to *Modernismo*, proposing we rethink the place of the movement among world literatures and vis-à-vis Spanish literature. Lastly, Mariano Siskind's *Cosmopolitan Desires: Global Modernity and World Literature in Latin America* (2014), whose ideas I discuss in Chapter 1, puts forth a wide-ranging reevaluation of the discourse of cosmopolitanism in Latin American literature, relating it to world literatures and discourses of modernity from a comparative perspective. In his work, he analyzes Darío's notion of world literature and his relationship to French literature by closely reading overlooked texts from the debates of the early years of *Modernismo* and Darío's late poetry.

Perhaps the most recent notable development is the collaborative program AR.DOC (Archivo Rubén Darío Ordenado y Centralizado), which is currently preparing a digital corpus of Darío-related documents, in addition to an authoritative edition of Darío's complete works in twenty volumes to be published by 2026. The project is spearheaded by scholars Rodrigo Caresani and Daniel Link of the National University of Tres de Febrero in Argentina, in collaboration with other researchers from institutions such as Harvard University and the *Ibero-Amerikanisches Institut* of Berlin, bringing together Darío scholars from across the globe.

The scholarship discussed above offers a picture of Darío as a man of letters writ large, not solely a poet. Over the course of the twentieth century, the notion of Darío as an eminently Francophile poet gradually gave way to an understanding of his writing that included his engagement with literature from the Americas, alongside Early Modern, Medieval, and Classical Literature. Darío's work as a short-story writer was brought to the fore. Then, in the 1960s and 1970s, Darío as the first modern Spanish American writer who suffered from, and wrote about, all the cultural anxieties of his time came to prominence: Darío the professional writer, the literary critic, and the cultural commentator. This perspective was complemented by later studies that further probed the political and cultural dimensions of his writings, facilitating the availability of works that had otherwise remained in obscurity. From the 2000s on, the focus seems to have shifted onto Darío as cosmopolitan traveler.

Unlike many of the works listed above, this book proposes that a more meaningful return to Darío's poetry is now overdue. It presents a comprehensive analysis of Darío's afterlife in English, seeking to answer the question of a major writer's obscurity in the Anglophone world. Also, it uncovers the multilingualism of Darío's poetry, which has been ignored by critics. What I mean by multilingualism is the presence of languages other than Spanish in Darío's oeuvre, both in the shape of the poems he wrote in French, as well as in the use of aspects of other languages which he instilled into his poetry (a wide use of Gallicisms, Latinate Spanish words, Catalan, Provençal poetic forms, among others). Multilingualism is by no means something radical or groundbreaking in literature.[23] From the times of the Augustan poets, writers have cultivated more than one language to different ends.[24] If it might not seem that way, it's for ideological reasons which are summarized neatly by Claudio Guillén as follows:

> Sentada por una parte en el nacionalismo excluyente y centralizador, y por otra en el concepto romántico del alma o genio inconfundible de cada idioma, [la literatura comparada] no atendió con suficiente simpatía a los fenómenos de multilingüismo, tan importantes a lo largo de toda la historia literaria de Occidente.[25]

Surprisingly, the first modern, scholarly approaches to multilingualism in literature can be found in two articles from as recently as the 1960s.[26] However, as we move further away from Romanticist notions of literature, and so-called globalization follows its course, multilingualism in literature should become more apparent.[27]

Translation as a Critical Tool

In the increasingly global world of academia, over the past decades the term "translation" has taken center stage in literary debates of various kinds: comparative literature, postcolonial literature, world literature(s), cultural studies, intermedia studies, etc.[28] It has proven to be extraordinarily flexible for metaphor, particularly when the term is used with a focus on its etymology—from the Latin *translatio*, which denotes a carrying or moving across of something—since it emphasizes movement across space or time, enabling a wider use of the concept. In the case of Spanish and French, the two other main languages which are used in this book, the etymology of the term is slightly different: *traducción* and *traduction* come from the Latin *traductio*, which mainly denotes to pass or to cross from one place to another, as opposed to moving something across.[29] *Traductio* also means the public shaming of someone or the exposure of someone to public ridicule (a meaning which is partially preserved in the English verb "to traduce"). As this book shows, the role of translation within literature already is multifarious and complex. While metaphorical notions of translation (such as cultural translation) can certainly be useful in identifying traits or patterns among cultures that would otherwise remain unseen, they run the risk of ignoring the complexities of translation "proper."[30] As Borges suggests, thinking about translation touches on issues that are at the heart of literature itself. In the case of the study of Darío, such issues reveal aspects of his writing which have been overlooked: both its multilingualism and the historical and cultural questions it raises regarding the shifting status of Spanish American literature in English.

As the title indicates, in this book I "use" translation to read Darío's poetry. This implies a use of the term that goes beyond merely looking at how Darío has been translated (which I do in Chapter 3).[31] It means also reading the work of Rubén Darío the translator, looking at how he creatively incorporates other texts and languages alongside his Spanish. As I explain further in Chapter 1, though Darío translated several texts in the traditional sense of the term, his most interesting use of translation appears in his own poetry.

A translator is someone who reads a text being mindful of the relationship between two languages which are in tension: the language in which the text is written and the virtual language into which they will render it. In the case of Darío, it's well known that he was greatly influenced by French language and literature. To read Darío through translation also means being cognizant of his relationship to French in order to understand how it shaped his Spanish. As I explain in Chapters 1 and 2, reading with this focus in mind reveals not only how Darío translates, but how he glosses, rewrites, annotates, and expands on French writers in his own poetry. It shows how the Nicaraguan author uses other languages or dialects in his writing, namely Provençal, Early Modern Spanish, Catalan, and Latin. While his engagement with these languages is less intense than it is with French, they all fill his writing with echoes or resonances from other authors and traditions.

Owing to the monolingualism of Spanish American criticism, the multilingualism of Darío's writing has gone unremarked over the years, despite the vast amount of scholarship his writing has inspired. No one has looked at how the presence of several languages can be found in Darío's writing. When his relation to another language has indeed been studied, critics have focused on the relation between Darío's writing and solely one language, as in the case of Erwin K. Mapes's *L'influence française dans l'œuvre de Rubén Darío*. But even then, due to conceptual limitations inherent in notions such as that of literary influence, as well as an understanding of imitation as something opposed to originality, the complexity and sophistication of Darío's engagement with French writers has not been adequately studied. The "influence" of French literature on Darío escapes the Bloomian model in which one "strong" poet influences "weaker" ones, as his use of his French counterparts is deliberate and strategic. As I specify in Chapter 1, Darío chooses his influences to perform a literary persona that acquires prestige from the names to which it alludes, creating a genealogy that corresponds to his vision of Spanish American literature. The ways he borrows, translates, rewrites, combines, abridges, and expands on his sources show how the originality of Darío's style is inextricable from imitation. As he himself avers in a passage to which I come back throughout this book:

> *Qui pourrais-je imiter pour être original ?* me decía yo. Pues a todos. A cada cual le aprendía lo que me agradaba, lo que cuadraba a mi sed de novedad y a mi delirio de arte: los elementos que constituirían después un medio de manifestación individual. Y el caso es que resulté original.[32]

The passage comes from Darío's response to Franco-Argentine writer Paul Groussac, who had criticized him for his lack of originality in relation to his

French sources. Groussac ends his own article in an ironic tone, using the quotation above—"Qui pourrais-je imiter pour être original ?", taken from French writer François Coppée—to deride the young Nicaraguan poet's alleged lack of originality. Darío answers by turning the question on its head, recasting it as the departure point for any writer's quest for originality. In a proto-Borgesian sense, for Darío the only originality possible is in the way we imitate.[33]

Reading Darío through translation obviously also means looking at other translations of his writing published to date. In this sense, the rendering of any author leads a translator to engage with previous translations. Over time, such renderings come to consolidate a tradition unto themselves (a micro-canon of sorts) which in turn can be read for traces or reflections of the predominant poetics of the period in which they were produced. As I explain in Chapter 3, while I discuss in detail the role of anthologies and periodicals in Darío's afterlife, in my close readings I focus mostly on book-length translations of Darío in English. Though important for the genre of poetry, periodicals have a limited reach in creating a readership for a translated author beyond specialized circles. On the other hand, as I show in the chapter, book publications are a good measure of the prestige a foreign author commands in a literary culture.

I focus on English-language translations because many of the world's most influential universities are in predominantly Anglophone countries. Also, the canon of World Literature is articulated in English. While undeniable, this fact is deeply problematic for the inherent diversity of the literatures of the world. One way of addressing this imbalance is to raise questions regarding the invisibility of certain works and to probe into their relation to translation, not least when the work is that of a canonical writer from a major literary tradition, as in the case of Rubén Darío and Spanish.

Nevertheless, a rigorous approach to the question of Darío's obscurity in English reveals that it's not enough to look at the quality of certain translations and assess their success in rendering the Nicaraguan poet's texts. To answer the question thoroughly, one must investigate not only the history of the translation of poetry in English, but also the history of Spanish American literature in English. In this sense, the question of translating Darío is a historical one.

After exploring the role of translation in Darío, I move on to the analysis of Darío in translation. In Chapter 3, I look at Darío's work vis-à-vis the history of the translation of Spanish American literature. This leads me to the analysis of the first efforts to translate Spanish American poetry in the United States, which took place in the early decades of the twentieth century under the aegis of Pan-Americanism and Good Neighbor Policy. I discuss the contribution of important though largely forgotten figures such as Salomón de la Selva, Alice Blackwell, and H. R. Hays during these years, who paved the way for later translators. I consider the case of Chilean poet Gabriela Mistral's afterlife in English as a point of comparison for Darío. Despite being the first Latin American Nobel laureate, and one of the first women in the history of the prize, Mistral died without having a book publication under her name in English. I comment on the possible reasons and conditions that led to those circumstances, considering the context of the publishing landscape of Latin American literature. Mistral's case confirms that periodicals and anthology publications have a limited effect in creating a new readership for a foreign author, thus helping us piece together the puzzle of Darío's obscurity.

Since the manner in which translation tends to be done in a literary culture reflects its dominant poetic norms, I also analyze the differences between Modernism and *Modernismo*, the latter of which has often been problematically called Hispanic Modernism or, in some cases, Modernism *tout court*.[34] This is tantamount to suggesting that they are roughly equivalent literary movements—a notion that fails to account for the historical and cultural nuances that distinguish them, the consequences of which bear heavily on the reception of authors like Darío. To flesh out these nuances, I discuss Arthur Symons's reading of the *fin de siècle* in *The Symbolist Movement in Literature* (1899) and compare it to Darío's in *Los raros* (1898)—two works by authors who were among the most important cultural mediators of their time—with the aim of drawing out the consequences for how poetics in English and Spanish would develop differently thereafter. I analyze how Darío reacts to certain avant-garde or proto-avant-garde works by Filippo Tommaso Marinetti, Arthur Rimbaud, and Auguste Rodin. As I explain in the chapter, Darío's rejection or puzzlement in looking at the work of these artists illustrates what Beatriz Colombi, following Homi K. Bhabha, calls *modernidades desfasadas*. The discussion of Modernism and *Modernismo* as two expressions of modernity separated by a *desfasamiento* or historical lag, both as a result of cultural differences as well as of the various and uneven processes of modernization which each context underwent, serves the purpose of illuminating the literary evolution that led to the nearly nonexistent reception of, for example, Salomón de la Selva and Thomas Walsh's *Eleven Poems* (1916), the first book-length translation of Darío in English.

I then trace the changes that English-language translation poetics underwent over the course of the twentieth century, touching on how the Deep Image poets, as a reaction to Modernism, used translation to incorporate new elements that would reinvigorate US poetry. I analyze the cultural implications of some of their appropriative renderings of Spanish American poets such as César Vallejo and Pablo Neruda. While their translation practices remain problematic and are at times even clumsy, they created a new readership for Spanish-language poetry in translation, to the extent that the Latin American poetry anthology rose to be a minor genre in and of itself. For that reason, based on the research of Scott Douglas Challener and others, I comment on the role of the translation anthology in relation to US post-war literature and its relevance for Darío's afterlife.

During the 1960s, after almost forty years of no book publication of Darío, Lysander Kemp published *Selected Poems of Rubén Darío* (1965). The analysis of the context of Kemp's reception inevitably broaches the influence of the so-called "Boom" of Spanish American literature from the 1960s on. As I explain, the way Darío is received in those years can be seen as illustrative of the preconceptions and expectations on the part of Anglophone readers of what Spanish American literature looks like. Likewise, it shows how Darío's literary modernity, once so groundbreaking in one literary culture, would quickly seem outdated when read according to Anglophone modernist aesthetics.

I then focus on the scholarly translations that have appeared, after another hiatus of almost forty years, in roughly the last two decades: Will Derusha and Alberto Acereda's *Selected Poems of Rubén Darío: A Bilingual Anthology* (2001), Stanley Appelbaum's *Stories and Poems/Cuentos y Poesías: A Dual-Language Book* (2002), Derusha and Acereda's full translation of Darío's *Cantos de vida y esperanza*, rendered as *Songs of Life and Hope* (2004); finally,

Rubén Darío: Selected Writings (2006) translated by Andrew Hurley, Greg Simon, and Steven White, as part of the Penguin Classics series.[35] I look at what these translators have to say about translation and about their approach to translating Darío in order to elucidate their choices and strategies. Moreover, I cite the different ways in which these translators have rendered the same poem, to give concrete examples of their approaches. Ultimately, what emerges from this second section of the book is that the translation of literature is only superficially about language. Cultural and historical differences between literary cultures bear more heavily on it.

Finally, I include a Coda at the end of the volume in which I explore Darío's poetics of *(h)armonía*. I discuss what Darío scholars have said about the topic and apply those critical insights to an exercise in translation of the poem "Ama tu ritmo" from *Prosas profanas* (1898). This last section hints at a way forward from the translation strategies that so far have failed to render the *modernista*'s poems successfully. It shows how ad hoc translation strategies which prioritize the main features of a text can be elaborated through the understanding and application of a writer's poetics.

Overview

As has been elucidated over the course of this Introduction, in this book I apply the notion of translation to the reading of Rubén Darío's poetry in a twofold sense; it's therefore divided into two sections: "Translation in Darío" and "Darío in Translation."

The first section focuses on reading the work of the Nicaraguan author by analyzing the use of translation in his own poetry, thereby revealing the way in which other languages shaped his writing. It's comprised of two chapters: Chapter 1 "Thinking in French and Writing in Spanish" focuses on Darío's engagement with French writers; Chapter 2 "Not only from the Roses of Paris" looks at Darío's use of Early Modern Spanish, Provençal, Catalan, and Latin.

The second section focuses on how Darío has been translated into English. Specifically, Chapter 3 "English Translations of Rubén Darío" looks at translation as a historical issue by analyzing existing translations of Rubén

Darío and discussing the historical and literary circumstances of their reception from a comparative perspective. The section is followed by a Coda, "Translating Darío's Poetics of '(H)armonía'", which elucidates Darío's ideas around *armonía* to delve into his poetics and propose a new strategy for his translation that shows a way forward from those done until now.

Part One

Translation in Darío

1

Thinking in French and Writing in Spanish

Quite literally, Rubén Darío wanted to write in French. In an elegiac book called *A. de Gilbert*, written in 1889 for a deceased friend, he writes:

> Oh, cuántas veces en aquel cuarto, en aquellas heladas noches, él y yo, los dos soñadores, unidos por un afecto razonado y hondo, nos entregábamos al mundo de nuestros castillos aéreos! Iríamos á París, seríamos amigos de Armand Silvestre, de Daudet, de Catulle Mendes; le preguntaríamos á éste por qué se deja en la frente un mechón de su rubia cabellera; oiríamos á Renán en la Sorbona y trataríamos de ser asiduos contertulios de madama Adam; y escribiríamos libros franceses! eso sí.[1]

One year later, after the first edition of *Azul...* had sold out, a second edition appeared in Guatemala with added corrections and new writings. It now included Juan Valera's famous letters to Darío from 1888, which had conferred on the book and its author some renown. The true novelty, however, lay in that it included three poems in French, presented under the section "Echos": "Chanson Crépusculaire," "A Mademoiselle," and "Pensée." Unfortunately, Darío had made more than one metrical mistake in the poems, as he recognizes in his autobiography:

> Yo ignoraba cuando los escribí muchas nociones de poética francesa. Entre ellas, pongo por caso, el buen uso de la "e" muda, que, aunque no se pronuncia en la conversación, o es pronunciada escasamente según el sistema de algunos declamadores, cuenta como sílaba para la medida del verso.[2]

They were suppressed from subsequent editions. Despite the failure those three poems represented in Darío's endeavor to write in the language of Hugo, in 1896 (about six years later) he would argue against Paul Groussac that "Azul es un libro parnasiano, y por lo tanto, francés," after acknowledging that "mi sueño era escribir en lengua francesa. Y aún [sic] versos cometí en ella que merecen perdón porque no se ha vuelto a repetir."[3] Clearly, Darío suggests that his mistakes in French verse dissuaded him from further attempts to write in the language.

He would not publish in French again until 1907, after more than seven years in Paris, when a poem called "«Helda»" came out as part of the collection *El canto errante*. And he would only do so again seven years later, in 1914, when the poem "France-Amérique" was published in *Mundial*, the magazine he edited, thereafter included in the collection of the same year, *Canto a la Argentina y otros poemas*. As Mariano Siskind notes, the poem "has been utterly ignored by critics of *modernismo*."[4] It's especially noteworthy because it associates France with translation:

> Marseillaises de bronze et d'or qui vont dans l'air
> Sont pour nos cœurs ardents le chant de l'espérance.
> En entendant du coq gaulois le clairon clair
> On clame: Liberté ! Et nous traduisons: France ![5] (ll. 13–16)

For Siskind, the use of the term *traduisons* in the poem reveals how French translation is, in Darío's poetics, a condition for aesthetic modernity:

> Of course, Darío is not a French poet, and *Azul* and *Prosas profanas* are not, literally, French books. Their Frenchness results from an operation of translation. If France is immediately modern, in and for itself, in Darío's books of the 1890s [...] Latin America is modern *through* France—France as mediation, as the instance that enables a Latin American translation of modern forms, images, and desires. Darío's literature is *Latin Americanly French* [...] Darío returned to this idea of French translation as the condition that makes aesthetic modernity possible in Latin America toward the end of his life, after he had made Paris his adopted home, in a poem he wrote in French, "France-Amérique".[6]

While much of what Siskind argues is true when it comes to Darío's poetic aims of the 1890s, he overinterprets the term *traduisons*. If we read the whole text, it becomes clear that "France-Amérique" is an anti-war poem like many others Darío wrote late in life, around the time the First Great War began. Below is the stanza that immediately precedes the one above.

> Il semblerait que tous les démons du passé
> viennent de s'éveiller empoisonnant la terre.
> Si contre nous l'étendard sanglant s'est levé,
> c'est l'étendard hideux de ce tyran: la Guerre;[7] (ll. 9–12)

"Marseillaises de bronze et d'or" in line 13 turns out to be an allusion to the French Revolution, just like the mentions of "Liberté" (l. 16) and "Fraternité" (l. 25). Through its rhetorical flourishes painstakingly set in alexandrines, the poem suggests that the Americas and France join strengths to overcome war. The cry "France!," which is according to Darío how Spanish Americans translate "Liberté!," refers not to aesthetic but to political freedom granted by the social conquests of the French Revolution. Despite this, Siskind interprets these lines as an aesthetic commentary on the worldview of *Modernismo*:

> "On clame: Liberté! Et nous traduisons: France!": we translate France, *for* and *in* Latin America, and we translate liberty as France, and France as liberty. Darío's translational intervention makes France and freedom interchangeable, where freedom is understood as the pillar of the discourse of modernity and, in the case of Latin American *modernismo*, points to the idea of freedom from want and from aesthetic and cultural marginality. This, in turn, makes possible the nontransparent, nonmimetic translation that constitutes the *modernista* aesthetic formation.[8]

According to Darío's contemporary, Chilean writer Francisco Contreras, the poem was, however, written for a diplomatic occasion:

> Rubén Darío compuso estos versos para ser leídos en fiesta de una institución de carácter panamericano: el "Comité France Amérique" y acaso también en la secreta esperanza que el pobre poeta abrigaba todavía de volver a ser diplomático.[9]

Saavedra Molina explains that the poem was read in May 1914 and was then self-translated into Spanish as "Oda a la Francia" and published in the Cuban newspaper *El Fígaro* on October 4, 1914.[10] Still, it is curious that Darío chose the term *traduisons*. At the very least, it belies Darío's position vis-à-vis French culture as a Spanish-speaking immigrant living in Paris who must translate the francophone world around him.

We can use the term heuristically to think about Darío's relation to French. To go back to Darío's article in reply to Groussac, after having confessed that it was his dream to write in French, he writes that:

> Al penetrar en ciertos secretos de armonía, de matiz, de sugestión, que hay en la lengua de Francia, fué mi pensamiento descubrirlos en el español, o aplicarlos [...] Y he aquí como, pensando en francés y escribiendo en castellano que alabaran por lo castizo académicos de la Española, publiqué el pequeño libro que iniciaría el actual movimiento literario americano.[11]

It's revealing to look at Darío's so-called *galicismo mental* in the shadow of his failure to write in French. Not to regard it as a second-rate solution compared to writing in French proper, but to consider it in terms of literary traditions. When Darío claims that *Azul...* is a French book, though not being written in French, more than saying that it is "Latin Americanly French," as Siskind suggests, Darío seems to position himself within French literary tradition in spite of the language barrier. If his ambition was to live in Paris and to write in French, it's because he literally wanted to become a French-language writer. However, he failed. Instead, he wrote as if he were part of the tradition of French poetry, but did so in Spanish: He composed poems that engaged with French themes and motives and can be read as a direct response to them. In a letter to Miguel de Unamuno, he writes:

> Le confesaré, desde luego, que no me creo escritor *americano*. Esto lo he demostrado en cierto artículo que me vi forzado a escribir cuando Groussac me honró con una crítica. Mejor que yo ha desarrollado el asunto el señor Rodó, profesor de la Universidad de Montevideo. Le envío su trabajo. Mucho menos soy castellano. Yo ¿le confesaré con rubor? no pienso en castellano. Más bien pienso en francés. O mejor, pienso *ideográficamente*; de ahí que mi obra no sea castiza. Hablo de mis libros últimos. Pues los primeros, hasta *Azul*, proceden de innegable cepa española, al menos en la forma.[12]

The letter is remarkable despite the affectation. Darío is masquerading as someone who literally does not think in Spanish but in French, echoing Valera's claim regarding his style as the result of a *galicismo mental*.¹³ The somewhat theatrical claim can be construed as referring to Darío's literary intent to transpose French forms and motifs into Spanish, hence "ideographically." On the other hand, it's worth noting that this francophone guise was part of Darío's self-fictionalization as the hero of *Modernismo*, a literary persona he began to cultivate in the 1890s. As I analyze in greater depth in Chapter 2, this persona changed over time. Later in his life, particularly from 1905 on, Darío wrote of himself as an "hijo de América [...] nieto de España."¹⁴ In other words, he was not so French anymore, and fervently Hispanic instead. This was possibly a result of his failure to enter the literary milieu of Paris, which contrasted sharply with the admiration he inspired, and the stimulating intellectual exchanges he found, in Spain.

In any case, while Darío's relation to French language and culture was complex and had a history of its own, it was defined by translation, as the poem "France-Amérique" hints at. Naturally, before being able to read and write in French, Darío read francophone literature in translation. One of his first encounters with it was by way of a Spanish translation of Théophile Gautier made by the Nicaraguan writer Modesto Barrios. As Darío himself writes in a preface to Jesús Hernández Somoza's book *Historia de tres años del gobierno Sacasa* (1893): "Modesto Barrios traducía a Gautier y daba las primeras nociones del modernismo," revealing the translatory dimension of *Modernismo* as a movement.¹⁵ Ernesto Mejía Sánchez explains that Barrios was director of the National Library of Nicaragua (1882–5) when Darío was fifteen years old.¹⁶ This suggests that it was through translation that Darío first made contact with some of the French writers who were to influence him in his career. In *Historia de mis libros*, Darío comments on another French writer whom he first read in Spanish: "Fue Catulle Mendès mi verdadero iniciador, un Mendès traducido, pues mi francés todavía era precario."¹⁷

Translation appears to have been Darío's preferred method for learning French as an autodidact. In a letter written to Juan J. Cañas in 1886, he mentions: "El señor [Eduardo] Poirier habla con perfección francés, inglés y alemán. Yo he adelantado mucho en el francés, que hablo casi sin dificultad;

y el inglés lo traduzco y sigo estudiándolo."[18] In one of the least studied books of Darío's youth, *El salmo de la pluma* (a collection of poems published in newspapers from 1883 to 1889), there is a section called "Paráfrasis y traducciones," which includes rhymed translations of Henry Longfellow, Lord Byron, and Victor Hugo's *La Légende des siècles*. Since Hugo's presence is so prominent in all of Darío's later writings, the importance of translation can hardly be overstated: In his study of Spanish meter, Navarro Tomás states that the alexandrine in Spanish acquired different rhythms only after Darío's first translations of Hugo.[19] In addition, one of the poems included in *Azul…*, "Pensamiento de otoño," is itself a translation of the French poet Armand Silvestre.[20]

Were these translations only stepping stones in achieving a longed-for mastery of French, as the three poems of *Azul…* might suggest? It does not seem as simple as that. While Darío aspired to become a French-language writer, Spanish language was a political and literary concern for him as early as 1882. At the age of fifteen, he published an article titled "El idioma español" in the newspaper *El Porvenir de Nicaragua*. There Darío proposes some changes to the Spanish written in the Americas—"La necesidad i [sic] el uso han introducido en el idioma español diferencias remarcables, especialmente aquende del Atlántico"—and goes on to say that "muchas palabras modernas indispensables ya hasta en el estilo más elevado" lay outside "el gremio del habla española."[21] What we can safely assume is that Darío wanted to become a multilingual writer who could also write from within the French tradition. After all, the second edition of *Azul…* is a bilingual book, insofar as it includes writings in Spanish and French.

As with so many of Darío's political and literary views, Martí was a key influence for his insight into the possibilities of multilingualism. When Martí wrote about the Irish-Colombian poet Diego Fallon (1882), he advised his fellow Spanish Americans as follows:

> Para hablar bien nuestra lengua, no hay como conocer otras: el contraste nos enamora de la nuestra; y el conocimiento nos habilita para tomar de las ajenas lo que a la nuestra le haga falta, y curarnos de los defectos que ella tenga y en los demás estén curados.[22]

There is a similar ring in Darío's "Historia de mis libros":

> Y yo, que me sabía de memoria el «Diccionario de galicismos», de Baralt, comprendí que no sólo el galicismo oportuno sino ciertas particularidades de otros idiomas, son utilísimos y de una incomparable eficacia en un apropiado trasplante.[23]

If we seriously countenance Darío's assertion about knowing the dictionary by heart, it seems obvious that no one could have committed its pages to memory. Not only is it a colossal task, but a vain one from a literary point of view: Baralt's dictionary has vast amounts of useless information. On the other hand, however, the preface to the dictionary of Gallicisms is extremely interesting. In the opening pages, he warns the reader that an excessive use of Gallicisms in Spanish would lead to a new language, altogether different from both Spanish and French:

> Si continúan como hasta hoy y se van extendiendo estas y otras varias especies de galicismos; si seguimos tomando del francés palabras de buen ó mal sonido, y olvidamos por ellas las de uso corriente; si á las voces castellanas que conservemos se aplica significación que nunca tuvieron; y al formar la oración gramatical y el período distribuimos y enlazamos los términos de otra manera que la usual hasta ahora; el feliz resultado de tantas y tan graves innovaciones habrá de ser la formación de un idioma nuevo.[24]

From *Azul...* (1888) on, that is exactly what Darío would do. It does not seem far-fetched to surmise that Darío may have found, in Baralt's preface, either the formula for a new style or its confirmation. As the fifteen-year-old Darío knew well, the Spanish language needed a change: he would find that change in French language by way of creative translation.

While Darío gave up on writing in French, he found a way of writing in Spanish that used French calques and borrowings in what would signify a renovation of Spanish-language literature. As we will see later, he imbued Spanish with echoes of French. His writing became, in a sense, multilingual. Because Darío wanted to be read from the vantage point of French literature, his vision of literary history goes beyond any type of national boundary. As Siskind correctly notes,

These books [*Los raros* and *Prosas profanas*] display the desire for a literature configured around a French archive of poetic figures, syntaxes, and topics, whose perceived universality would allow it to be inscribed in the imagined synchronicity of a global modernism that, to Darío in 1896, marginalized Latin America.[25]

While overtly Francophile, this "archive of poetic figures, syntaxes, and topics," however, is not exclusively French. In *Los raros*, two authors who wrote in French but were born in Latin America, Lautréamont and Augusto de Armas,[26] are included alongside Poe, Ibsen, Martí, Eugénio de Castro, and Nordau.

Because Darío's writing is multilingual, it's also multilayered insofar as it offers at least two experiences of reading. We can imagine the experience of a Spanish-language reader at the turn of the twentieth century: In Darío's poetry, Spanish must have appeared odd or even uncanny—its rules were bent and its vocabulary made strange. On the other hand, if that reader also had French, certain words, tropes, meters, and themes belonging to French language and literature would come through Darío's Spanish as echoes at once familiar and new. Within the wider context of Western literature, this twofold layer corresponds to two distinct ways of representing literary history. In the former, when Darío's oeuvre is read only from the locus of Spanish-language literary tradition, it seems to emerge as a groundbreaking body of work that renewed the literature of the language. In the latter, when the reader goes beyond national and linguistic boundaries, reading the Nicaraguan poet's oeuvre with French literary tradition in mind, a continuity across languages and traditions comes to the fore—which comprised what Darío called *el movimiento cosmopolita*, or in other words international Symbolism, which at the time was spreading across France, England, Italy, Portugal, Spain, and Spanish America.[27] Traditionally, Darío's oeuvre has mostly been read and represented only according to the former, even when recognizing its "debts" to and "influences" of French literature. The Peruvian critic Julio Ortega comments on this blind spot present in much Darío scholarship:

> Si bien Rubén Darío, como él mismo explica, se documentaba para escribir algunos poemas, el rastreo de sus fuentes ha ofrecido siempre una versión limitada de su proceso de composición. El problema de cómo leer esas

fuentes, a la luz del poema, no está resuelto, ni siquiera bien planteado, y cada vez que la crítica académica ha creído demostrar las referencias de un poema suyo, ha reincidido en la simplificación y hasta en cierta pobreza conceptual.[28]

The authorities on Darío's sources and influences—Arturo Marasso, Erwin K. Mapes, among others—study those sources as a means of explicating Darío's originality. Unlike them, I will explore the latter possibility of reading I have just described, by closely reading a selection of poems which best illustrate the rich conversation Darío held with his French counterparts.

Darío's Poetry as a Conversation with France

Before delving into the poems, it's worth remembering Derek Attridge's definition of "creative reading" as an articulation in words of a response to a text "as if the work being read demanded a new work in response."[29] The poems in which Darío rewrites Théophile Gautier, Théodore de Banville, Jules Barbey d'Aurevilly, and Paul Verlaine seem to fall within this kind of response—spurred by the fact that nothing quite like what these writers were doing in French existed in Spanish. The poems analyzed here appear to emerge as responses to the French literature of Darío's time. They are rewritings, rejoinders, glosses, versions, translations—displaying an engagement with their source that is reminiscent of what was formerly understood as *imitatio*.[30] To a certain degree, one could argue that this is a trait that all poets show in their work. As the poet and critic Craig Morgan Teicher explains,

> Poetry is a conversation, an extended one, occupying, perhaps, the span of an entire life. Poets converse, first and foremost, with their language [...] and with the idea of language itself.[31]

For poets like Darío, poetry is also a conversation with other languages. Teicher elaborates on how considering the conversational dimension of poetry might bear on how we conceive of literary influence:

> We tend to define poetic influence in terms of how a later poet is shaped by an earlier one. This definition perhaps oversimplifies what poetic influence is: the internalization and adaptation of other poets' work into a new style. Poetry is a reader's art: poets make poems in response to the poems they've read. [...] Poems take place in many kinds of conversations, whether with other poems and poets, with an imagined reader, with the culture at large, or with the poet's own previous, current, or future selves. [...] Poetic influence occurs as an aspect of these conversations, a volleying between poets living and dead.[32]

Teicher's musings on poetry as a reader's art are fitting for the poems that will be explored in this chapter.

To come back to French, Darío was fascinated by the language and culture. As far as literary success goes, Paris was almost literally heaven on earth for him. The following passage from his autobiography is well known:

> Yo soñaba con París, desde niño, al punto de que cuando hacía mis oraciones rogaba a Dios que no me dejase morir sin conocer París. París era para mí como un paraíso donde se respirase la esencia de la felicidad sobre la tierra. Era la ciudad del Arte, de la Belleza y de la Gloria; y, sobre todo, era la capital del Amor, el reino del Ensueño. E iba yo a conocer París, a realizar la mayor ansia de mi vida. Y cuando en la estación de Saint Lazare, pisé tierra parisiense, creí hollar suelo sagrado.[33]

His idealization of Paris was far from unique for his time, as Latin American culture pined for the symbolic capital of France. We can find parallels between Darío's relation to French and Silviano Santiago's description of the relation between the Latin American writer and European literature.[34] According to Santiago, because of their postcolonial predicament, European texts presented themselves as attractive and fascinating objects in themselves to Latin American writers. The books written in response to those texts ended up being a kind of global translation, pastiche, or digression, which reflects that fascination. Darío's relation to French can fruitfully be thought of, in Santiago's words, as "the story of a sensual experience with foreign signs." As we will see later, the Nicaraguan author shows a fascination with French words, to the extent of fetishizing and inscribing them into his writing as prestigious signs of cosmopolitanism. And if we are willing to broaden our notion of translation, the poems I will now analyze could effectively be thought of, in the words of Santiago, as a "global translation."

I will begin with poems from *Prosas profanas*. Although the texts of *Azul...* include elements I have mentioned as part of this second possibility of reading Darío's oeuvre, they do so to a lesser degree. In *Prosas profanas* there is a clear change regarding Darío's Spanish. Though the language of *Azul...* is already scattered with French words—*esmaragdin* appears as *esmaradigna* in "El rey burgués," *farandole* as *farandola* in "El velo de la reina Mab," *chartreuse* in "La ninfa," and so forth—for the most part, the vocabulary employed was already part of Spanish.[35] By contrast, a survey of *Prosas profanas* shows at least thirty-eight borrowings from the French. This does not include all the Greek words that Darío borrowed from Parnassian diction (Leconte de Lisle, one of the most influential poets of *Parnasse*, was a prolific translator of Classical Greek literature). Nor does it include the many words typical of the diction of *Romantisme*, which the Nicaraguan author most likely came to by way of Victor Hugo. Any reader of Darío would naturally recognize *d'or, sonore, vague, brume, harmonie, lyre, soupir, l'azur, l'aube,* and so forth, as familiar *modernista* terms.

While in *Azul...* Darío is writing from within the French tradition, his ambition seems to be to write in both languages. In *Prosas profanas*, however, he has given up for the time being on the dream of writing in French, and in turn has radically transposed elements of French language and literature into Spanish. One language is brushed against another.

Darío's Creative Rewritings

The poem "Canción de carnaval" is both a translation and a rewriting of a poem by Banville called "Mascarades," from the collection *Odes funambulesques* (1857). The title itself is telling: "Mascarades" is a poem about the famous carnival of Paris, a fact which sheds light on Darío's own choice of title "Canción de carnaval." What most critics have failed to recognize is that Banville's poem is not merely a source or an influence. In Santiago's terms, it is a "hegemonic" text that Darío, from the "periphery," creatively reads, translates, and rewrites.

The poem's epigraph, in fact, is a line from "Mascarades." By citing Banville, the poet is pointing the reader to the French text. Furthermore, in "Historia de mis libros" Darío acknowledges that "La Canción de Carnaval es también a lo Banville, una oda funambulesca, de sabor argentino, bonaerense."[36] It's a poem that is expected to be read in tandem with Banville. At the same time, Darío's text is more than a translation; it's a new poem that says things which Banville's does not. Darío freely translates many passages of Banville's poem, rewriting it with added Argentine elements and even with Banvillesque elements that transcend "Mascarades" and are found elsewhere in the Frenchman's poetry. Below is a parallel comparison of the corresponding fragments:

Musa, la *máscara* apresta,	Le *Carnaval* s'amuse !
ensaya un aire *jovial*	Viens le chanter, ma *Muse*,
y goza y ríe en la fiesta	Sur un rhythme *gaillard*
del *carnaval*. (ll. 1–4)	Du bon Ronsard ! (ll. 1–4)
Ríe en la danza que gira,	Chante ton dithyrambe
muestra la *pierna rosada*,	En laissant voir ta *jambe*
y suene, como una lira,	Et ton sein arrosé
tu carcajada. (ll. 5–8)	D'un feu *rosé*. (ll. 9–12)
Mueve tu espléndido *torso*	Mets ta *ceinture*, et *plaque*
por las calles pintorescas	*Sur le velours* d'un claque
y juega y *adorna* el corso	Les rubans querelleurs
con rosas frescas. (ll. 41–44)	*Jonchés de fleurs* ! (ll. 41–44)

I have emphasized the most evident parallelisms between the poems. In the first stanza, both speakers refer to a Muse, inviting her to enjoy the carnival each poem celebrates. Banville's *Muse* corresponds to Darío's *Musa*, *Carnaval* to *carnaval*, *gaillard* to *jovial*—in the first line, Darío inserts the word of Banville's original title, *máscara*. In the other stanzas Darío displaces the description he translates; instead of *feu rosé* he opts for *pierna rosada*; in the third he writes *torso* in lieu of *ceinture*, and *adornar* instead of *joncher*. Darío also "translates" the meter: the Spanish lines are longer, but he keeps the abridged fourth line of each stanza to preserve the playful rhythm of Banville's *Odes funambulesques*. He also changes the rhyme scheme: while Banville's is AABB, Darío opts for ABAB.

As mentioned earlier, Darío also includes characters found in other poems by Banville: *Pierrot, Polchinelle* (which Darío translates as *Pulchinela*), *Colombine* (*Colombina*), *Arlequin* (*Arlequín*), and *le Clown* (*un clown*). Mapes has imaginatively described this as the result of Darío not finding Banville's poem Banvillesque enough for his own version.[37] However, Mapes plainly considers it "une imitation des *Mascarades*," in which Darío "reproduit admirablement l'impression donnée par le poème de Banville, mais comme nous l'avons dit, c'est le Banville de tous les poèmes de carnaval qu'il imite, plutôt que les *Mascarades* seules."[38] Marasso also calls it an imitation.[39] What leads both Mapes and Marasso to read the poem merely as such is their disregard of the Argentine elements that Darío includes in his version of Banville. For instance, in the fourth stanza we find:

Y que en tu boca risueña
que se une al alegre coro,
deje la abeja porteña
    su miel de oro. (ll. 13–16)

Later on, in the tenth and twelfth stanzas:

Sé lírica y sé bizarra
con la cítara sé griega;
O gaucha, con la guitarra
    de Santos Vega. (ll. 37–40)

De perlas riega un tesoro
de Andrade en el regio nido,
y en la hopalanda de Guido,
    polvo de oro. (ll. 45–48)

Darío includes, on the one hand, *lo porteño*; on the other, he inserts three allusions that change the meaning of the poem. The allusion to "la guitarra / de Santos Vega" refers to the poem "Santos Vega" by Rafael Obligado from 1885; the reference to Andrade alludes to the poet Olegario Víctor Andrade, whereas Guido is the poet Carlos Guido Spano.[40] All three poets are important figures of Argentine Romanticism. In that sense, Darío's Banvillesque muse will not only be *griega* but *gaucha*, as the mythical Santos Vega was, and will embellish the works of Andrade and Guido with *perlas* and *polvo de oro*. Contrary to what Mapes and Marasso claim, Darío is not merely imitating Banville. The bawdy gaiety of the Frenchman's muse, which celebrates France as opposed to other nations, becomes in the hands of Darío the muse of new poetry, which carries the accents of French verse to improve on its Argentine predecessors. Clearly, this is not purely imitation: Darío is translating and rewriting Banville to produce new meaning. What's more, he does so overtly, pointing the reader to the elements from the French text that are used in his own, as to have his poem read in conversation with its French counterpart. In the text we can also hear echoes of Banville's *Odes funambulesques*: many of its most colorful characters parade before our eyes. However, this is a Spanish-speaking Banville that does not celebrate the exquisiteness of French culture. Instead, it speaks of Argentine literature to come, mixing high and popular culture.

We find another case of rewriting in the poem "Bouquet." Unlike "Canción de carnaval," here Darío conceptually rewrites another poem. To begin with, the title itself is a Gallicism. As with the previous poem, in the first stanza Darío points the reader to the author whose writing he will cast anew:

> Un poeta egregio del país de Francia
> que con versos áureos alabó el amor
> formó un ramo harmónico, lleno de elegancia,
> en su *Sinfonía en Blanco Mayor*. (ll. 1–4)

He is referring to Théophile Gautier, the title of whose poem "Symphonie en blanc majeur" he translates for the reader. Commenting on Darío's use of intertextuality in this poem, Alberto Julián Pérez notes that Darío informs the reader of the poetic school of his text, creating an intertextual weaving with the French literary tradition represented by Parnassianism, as if the model text were a modifiable code that can be continued by others.[41] Though the intertextuality is undeniable, there is more to it than meets the eye. The poem continues as follows:

> Yo por ti formara, Blanca deliciosa,
> el regalo lírico de un blanco bouquet,
> con la blanca estrella, con la blanca rosa
> que en los bellos parques del azul se ve. (ll. 5–8)

As Julián Pérez notes, Darío establishes a continuity: Gautier wrote *un ramo harmónico* and he in turn will write *un blanco bouquet*. The reader is made complicit in his witnessing of this volleying between one poet and the other. However, significant differences separate the two. In his poem, Gautier explores the semantic possibilities of the color white, seemingly covering its whole connotative spectrum. From:

> De ces femmes il en est une,
> Qui chez nous descend quelquefois,
> Blanche comme le clair de lune
> Sur les glaciers dans les cieux froids; (ll. 9–12)

To:

> Sphinx enterré par l'avalanche,
> Gardien des glaciers étoilés,
> Et qui, sous sa poitrine blanche,
> Cache de blancs secrets gelés ? (ll. 68–71)

He does so not only through the repetition of the word *blanche*, but by extending it through metaphors that entail glaciers, snow, camellias, boreal regions, swans, satin, among other indicators of whiteness. It's a virtuosic display of poetic skill. Also, he uses those metaphors to describe a fabled *femme-cygne* from *les contes du Nord* (ll. 1–4), Scandinavia occupying a place of mythical exoticism. By contrast, Darío's poem is simpler, as it seems to use repetition and alliteration of a single word, namely "blanca," as the generative force of the poem.[42] Though the echoes of "Symphonie en blanc majeur" can be heard in "Bouquet," Darío's poem is notably less rich in metaphors. However, despite the appearance of flippancy, he takes intertextuality a step further: he does not merely create poetic continuity between one poem and another, as Pérez suggests, but answers to Gautier's last stanza with a rejoinder in his own poem. Gautier's poem ends with the following lines:

> Sous la glace où calme il repose,
> Oh ! qui pourra fonder ce cœur !
> *Oh ! qui pourra mettre un ton rose*
> *Dans cette implacable blancheur !* (ll. 69–72; emphasis added)

To which Darío writes:

> Yo, al enviarte versos, de mi vida arranco
> la flor que te ofrezco, blanco serafín.
> *¡Mira cómo mancha tu corpiño blanco
> la más roja rosa que hay en mi jardín!* (ll. 17–20; emphasis added)

I have emphasized the last two lines of each stanza to foreground Darío's ingenious rewriting of Gautier. Clearly, only the multilingual reader who has access to both texts in their original language can be complicit in Darío's mischievous turn: while Gautier presents the whiteness of his *femme-cygne* as immaculate and unattainable for its mythic quality, rhetorically asking who could change its cold whiteness to a mellow *rose*, Darío claims that *he* will stain the immaculate white with his reddest rose—a symbol of sensuality, voluptuousness, and desire. As with "Canción de carnaval," the term "imitation" falls short in describing what takes place between the two texts. Darío clearly writes a less ambitious poem, taking only what most interests him from Gautier; that is, the rhythmic qualities of repetition rather than its imagistic possibilities. However, after pointing the reader to the French text, as to show how the poem is meant to be read, Darío inserts a rejoinder to Gautier at the end of his poem.

The second poem of the subsection "Verlaine" called "El canto de la sangre" presents a similar case. Again, because it is placed under a subsection titled "Verlaine," the reader knows where to turn their eye for references and allusions. As with Gautier, here Darío takes from Verlaine what he is most interested in: the structure and use of repetition in a poem from *Sagesse* (1880), called "Voix de l'Orgueil: un cri puissant comme d'un cor." In Verlaine's poem, each stanza begins with a different "voice":

> Voix de l'Orgueil: un cri puissant comme d'un cor (l. 1)
> Voix de la Haine: cloche en mer, fausse, assourdie (l. 4)
> Voix de la Chair: un gros tapage fatigué (l. 8)
> Voix d'Autrui: des lointains dans des brouillards. Des noces (l. 12)

Darío uses the same structure to write a different poem:

> Sangre de Abel. Clarín de las batallas. (l. 1)
> [...] Sangre del Cristo. El órgano sonoro. (l. 4)

[…] Sangro de los martirios. El salterio. (l. 8)
[…] Sangre que vierte el cazador. El cuerno. (l. 12)

He further extends the device for three stanzas more. Where Verlaine writes about different voices, Darío writes about different episodes of blood-spilling. Where the former uses a colon to structure the beginning of each stanza, the latter uses a full stop, cutting the line in two. As with "Bouquet" and its echoes of Gautier, the echo of Verlaine here is not so much a resonance as a *déjà vu*, as it were, inspired by the form of the poem and its devices. This kind of relation is common to all poetry, which, as Morgan Teicher explains, is a conversation of sorts. However, what is unique in Darío is both the lineage he deliberately seeks to create by likening his writings to these poets—recall his phrase "Azul es un libro parnasiano, y por lo tanto, francés"—as well as the dialogue it seeks to open with its French counterparts.

Otherwise, there are no great parallelisms between the two texts. However, it is curious to note that a poem which openly uses the structure of a Verlainean text is included, as mentioned earlier, under a subsection titled "Verlaine." By being placed next to "Responso," "Canto de la sangre" also seems to pay homage to Verlaine—not by extolling the figure of the French poet like the former does, but by directly writing a Verlainean poem. Such homage is telling of the reading practices of the *modernistas*: Verlaine represents not only an influential poet, but new poetic forms to be learned and put into practice.

Further on in the collection we find a poem titled "Cosas del Cid." Here Darío rewrites Jules Barbey d'Aurevilly's poem "Le Cid" from the collection *Poussières* (1897), expanding the story that takes place therein. At this point we can see a pattern emerge: when Darío rewrites his French counterparts, he often abridges the text, aiming for synthesis. This is also the case of "Canción de carnaval," "Bouquet," and "Canto de la sangre." In this instance, Darío retells the story of Barbey's Cid in twenty-five lines, whereas Barbey's poem is fifty-eight lines long. However, in his retelling Darío glosses on Barbey's poem and, in a way, corrects it. This is the first stanza of the poem:

Cuenta Barbey, en versos que valen bien su prosa,
una hazaña del Cid, fresca como una rosa,
pura como una perla. No se oyen en la hazaña
resonar en el viento las trompetas de España, (ll. 1–4)

Again, Darío tells the reader what his source is. After praising the poem, Darío relates how Barbey's Cid is nonetheless devoid of the Hispanic context in which the story of *El Cid* originally takes place. To correct this lack, Darío includes contextual information of *El Cantar del mio Cid* in his rewriting of Barbey's story. The poem continues as follows,

> ni el azorado moro las tiendas abandona
> al ver al sol el alma de acero de Tizona.
> Babieca, descansando del huracán guerrero,
> tranquilo pace, mientras el bravo caballero (ll. 5–8)

And then,

> Rodrigo de Vivar pasa, meditabundo,
> por una senda en donde, bajo el sol glorioso,
> tendiéndole la mano, le detiene un leproso. (ll. 12–14)

Unlike Barbey, who other than "le Cid" only calls his hero "Campéador," Darío includes proper names in his poem to underline El Cid's Spanishness: Tizona, the name of his mythical sword; Babieca, his horse; and Rodrigo de Vivar, El Cid's real name. Once the retelling of Barbey's poem is complete, he adds the following segue:

> Tal es el sucedido que el Condestable escancia
> como un vino precioso en su copa de Francia.
> Yo agregaré este sorbo de licor castellano: (ll. 26–28)

The poem then includes another story, now entirely Darío's creation, in which El Cid meets "una niña que fuera un hada, o que surgiera/encarnación de la divina Primavera." (ll. 44–5) Iris M. Zavala explains how the meaning of El Cid's heroic deed is transformed in Darío's extension of the story: the encounter with "La Primavera" would be a symbolic version of the famous episode in which the girl from Burgos appears in the first part of the medieval poem. In Zavala's reading, Darío reappropriates Barbey's heroic, medieval, and sober style, and turns it into an evocative and suggestive one: "No busca la gesta del guerrero. En su poema el Cid se convierte en *el poeta.*"[43]

As with most of the previous poems, "Cosas del Cid" is not only an original creation, but also a gloss, a translation, and a rewriting of another poem. It was written after the Spanish–American War in 1898, during Darío's travels to Spain and France as a reporter for *La Nación*. It's no coincidence, then, that Darío is expanding his conversation with French poetry by including Spanish themes, motifs, and history in his writing.

"El reino interior" is a complex text that requires some unpacking. In the poem, the poet's soul, which is personified as a damsel in distress, is trapped inside a terrible tower that represents the poet's body. From the height of that tower she witnesses the encounter of the seven Virtues (embodied by seven princesses) and the seven deadly Sins (seven princes). Virtues and Sins do not clash in Manichean combat, however, as one would expect: they join one another amorously in the woods nearby. The poet's soul then goes back to sleep and expresses, in her dreams, a desire to have both Virtues and Sins embrace her.

The rewriting and translation here are intricate. To begin with, the poem has a dedication to Eugénio de Castro alongside an epigraph by Edgar Allan Poe, " ... with Psychis [*sic*], my soul!," ostensibly from the poem "Ulalume." Both these writers' qualities are extolled in *Los raros*. Judging from what Darío writes on de Castro in that book, he sees in him a spiritual brother in the sacred art of poetry:

> Leí sus versos. Desde el primer momento reconocí su iniciación en el nuevo sacerdocio estético, y la influencia de maestros como Verlaine. Y en veces su voz era tan semejante a la voz verleniana, que junté en mi imaginación el recuerdo de de Castro, al del amado y malogrado Julián del Casal, un cubano que era por cierto el hijo espiritual de *Pauvre Lelian*.[44]

Darío goes on to quote extensively from de Castro's *Sagramor* (1895), a long poem in which, as in "El reino interior," the speaker is tempted by external voices to commit sinful acts.[45] Therefore, as is habitual in Darío, by dedicating the poem to de Castro he is putting forth a lineage according to which he, along with the Portuguese poet, follow in the steps of Verlaine as continuers of "el renacimiento latino."[46] In addition to the epigraph, the personification of the poet's soul also seems to come from Poe. Three other names stand out in the poem: "fra Doménico Cavalca" (l. 3), "el divino Sandro" (ll. 35), and "los satanes verlenianos de Ecbatana" (ll. 44).

Fra Domenico Cavalca, an Italian friar from the thirteenth century, like Poe and de Castro, also appears in *Los raros*.[47] In the poem, Darío tells the reader to imagine the atmosphere he is describing as similar to that of Cavalca's writing, "cual la que pinta fra Doménico Cavalca / en sus Vidas de santos [...]" (ll. 4–5). The poet takes what he loves most as a reader and integrates it into his writing.[48] Francisco López Estrada, in his study *Rubén Darío y la edad media* (1971), links the figure of Cavalca to the influence of Pre-Raphaelitism on Darío. According to López Estrada, for the Pre-Raphaelites, Cavalca would represent something like the counterpart of Dante, which Darío readily incorporated into his writing.[49] In effect, in "Historia de mis libros" Darío writes that, in "El reino interior," "se siente la influencia de la poesía inglesa, de Dante Gabriel Rosétti [*sic*] y de algunos de los corifeos del simbolismo francés."[50] The description of the author's soul in the poem is similar to that of Rosetti's damozel in "The Blessed Damozel,"

> The blessed damozel lean'd out
> From the gold bar of Heaven (ll. 1–2)
> [...] She had three lilies in her hand,
> And the stars in her hair were seven (ll. 5–6).

For the sake of comparison, here are the lines from "El reino interior":

> Mi alma frágil se asoma a la ventana obscura
> de la torre terrible en que ha treinta años sueña. (ll. 10–11)
> [...] Y las manos liliales agita, como infanta
> real en los balcones del palacio paterno. (ll. 18–19)

Regarding ll. 18–19, Alfonso García Morales mentions Albert Samain's opening poem to his début collection *Au jardin de l'Infante* (1893), an author acclaimed in France at the time and would later be a decisive influence on Darío's protégé, Leopoldo Lugones.[51] The poem's title is the same as its first line: *Mon âme est une infante en robe de parade*. The coincidence between "infante" and "infanta" points to a more than likely relation. Darío seems to take the image from Samain and use it in his own poem. Moreover, by replacing Rosetti's damozel with the feminine figure of his own soul, he rewrites Rosetti: "the gold bar of Heaven" becomes "la torre terrible" of the poet's body, while the "three lilies in her hand" fancifully turns into "las manos liliales" of the poet's soul, using a neologism that retains some of the original English spelling (lilies/liliales), also found in de Castro's poems. On the other hand, "el divino Sandro" (l. 35) and "los satanes verlenianos de Ecbatana" (l. 44) are references to Sandro Botticelli and Verlaine's poem "Crimen amoris" from *Jadis et naguère* (1884). As we will see, the setting of "El reino interior" is a hybrid of Botticelli's "La Primavera" and Verlaine's "Crimen amoris." This is how Darío alludes to the former:

> La gentil Primavera, primavera le augura.
> [...] Como al compás de un verso, su paso suave rigen,
> tal el divino Sandro dejara en sus figuras
> esos graciosos gestos en esas líneas puras. (l. 12; ll. 34–36)

How do we know that "el divino Sandro" is an allusion to Botticelli? In the piece that Darío writes on Cavalca in *Los raros*, he says the following:

> No tengo conocimiento de que se haya traducido a nuestra lengua ningún libro del «primitivo» Fra Domenico Cavalca, en cuyas obras en prosa y en verso brilla la luz sencilla y adorable, la expresión milagrosa de las pinturas de un Botticelli [...] Si la pintura «primitiva» ha dado vuelo a la inspiración de los prerrafaelistas, la poesía, la literatura trecentista y cuatrocentista, resuena también en el laúd de Dante Gabriel Rosetti, en la lira de Swinburne.[52]

The passage further shows how *Los raros* and *Prosas profanas* are cut from the same cloth. In both the piece on Cavalca and "El reino interior" we find the same cluster formed by Pre-Raphaelitism, Cavalca, and Botticelli. The poem, therefore, turns out to be a case of *ekphrasis*: Darío transposes onto the poem the symmetrical composition of Botticelli's painting: on one side, white-hued characters (in Botticelli, the three Graces and Mercury; in Darío, the seven Virtues); and on the other side, contrasting characters (in Botticelli, dark Zephyr, and ornate Flora; in Darío, the seven crimson Sins). In between the two, Botticelli paints Venus, while Darío "paints" his Psyche. Marasso describes it as Darío reproducing with words what Botticelli did with colors in his *Primavera*. According to the critic, it would have been impossible for Darío to depict the seven crimson Sins the way he did had he not Botticelli's painting in sight.[53]

Darío imbues his poem with echoes of Verlaine's "Crimen amoris": "soie et or" resonates in "oro, seda"; "beaux demons" in "bellamente infernales"; "sept Péchés" in "siete poderosos Pecados"; "Ecbatane" in "Ecbatana"; and "sa couronne des fleurs" in "ciñen las cabezas triunfantes oro y rosas." Also, Darío surreptitiously alludes to Verlaine himself: "y en sus manos de ambiguos príncipes decadents" (l. 53).

Critics who have compared the two poems, such as Arturo Marasso, Alfonso García Morales, and Edmundo de Chasca,[54] have not paid sufficient attention to an important difference between them: while Darío's text sets the scene for a Manichean confrontation (which results in embrace rather than violence), Verlaine's text does not. What happens in Verlaine's whimsical text is a hecatomb that takes place outside a palace where only demons (not Virtues) have gathered. When one of those demons moves away from the group to give a speech, he *mentions* the need of a Manichean confrontation between Sins and Virtues:

> Nous avons tous trop souffert, anges et hommes,
> De ce conflit entre le Pire et le Mieux (ll. 44–45)
> [...] Ô vous tous, ô tous nous, ô les pécheurs tristes,
> Ô les gais Saints, pourquoi ce schisme têtu ? (ll. 48–49)
> [...] Assez et trop de ces luttes trop égales !
> *Il va falloir qu'enfin se rejoignent les*
> *Sept Péchés aux Trois Vertus Théologales* ! (ll. 52–54; emphasis added)

In the lines emphasized above, I believe we can find the origin of Darío's poem. "El reino interior" begins where "Crimen amoris" ends, but only to enact what the latter merely mentions as necessary. In this regard, the stanza of "El reino interior" in which Darío alludes to Verlaine's poem is especially revealing:

> Al lado izquierdo del camino y paralela-[55]
> mente, siete mancebos—oro, seda, escarlata,
> armas ricas de Oriente—, hermosos, parecidos
> a los satanes verlenianos de Ecbatana,
> vienen también [...] (ll. 41–45)

Marasso calls the allusion above "una señal de procedencia."⁵⁶ I would add that it is also a signal of destination. The poem invites us to reread Verlaine and then come back to it to read it again alongside Darío. It converses with its counterpart, instead of merely proceeding from it. As with Barbey's "Cosas del Cid," it expands Verlaine's poem and, from the perspective of Darío's poetics, improves on it. As seen in the lines quoted above, Verlaine's demon suggests joining the seven sins to the three theological virtues (namely Hope, Faith, and Charity). However, unlike Verlaine—and like Botticelli and the Pre-Raphaelites—Darío opts for symmetry by joining seven sins to seven virtues. The descriptions in "El reino interior" have a pictorial clarity to them, while those in "Crimen amoris" are deliberately blurry and suggestive. These differences between the poems are illustrative of the extent to which Darío is not imitating Verlaine but doing something altogether different. He is translating, rewriting, and annotating; he is rectifying what is not of his liking and bringing together other elements foreign to Verlaine's poetry to write a new text. The poem, in the end, is a tapestry of sorts in which sundry sources come together to form a whole: medieval hagiography, Verlainean moral conflict, Pre-Raphaelite representation of femininity, Poe-esque personification of the soul, and a Botticellian use of symmetry and proportion.

Strategies of Cosmopolitanism

At this point we can collate the common characteristics found in the texts analyzed so far. The starting point for these poems from *Prosas profanas* often seems to be another text, usually by a contemporary French poet. The poem is then translated and rewritten by Darío to cast it anew in Spanish. This usually entails some form of synthesis or pastiche. This second text is, nonetheless, loaded with French echoes. Therefore, the monolingual reader may recognize the presence of French literature in the words, names, and allusions of the poems; however, the multilingual reader will see in it glosses, translations, rewritings, rejoinders, corrections, annotations, among others. This is not to say that these poems must be exclusively read with their French counterpart in sight; yet when we do read them in this way, we can uncover the multilingual aspects of Darío's poetry that have been largely ignored by critics, perhaps due to the limitations of a framework that understands the relations between literary texts only in terms of plain and simple imitation. To fully grasp the sophistication of Darío's engagement with French poetry, we must read it in terms of what it does with its French sources, as this usually involves operations far too rich to be solely labeled "imitation" or "influence." As Santiago puts it:

> Can the work of art's originality be grasped if it is considered exclusively in terms of the artist's indebtedness to a model that was necessarily imported from the metropolis? Or, rather, would it not be more interesting to highlight the elements of the work that establish its difference?[57]

This limited framework fails to address the complex dynamics between these *modernista* poems and their French counterparts. One of the most revealing aspects of a poem by Darío is that there seems to be no desire to hide the sources that have given rise to the text. Quite the contrary: some poems seem to bear their allusions as marks of identity.[58] The reasons for this are related both to the readership Darío had in mind when he wrote his poetry, as well as to the literary tradition as part of which he wanted to be read.

In the first case, it's well known that a large network of literary magazines and journals spanned Latin America in Darío's time, publishing the latest European poetry both in its original language and in translation. Gerard Aching cogently likens this network to Darío's distillation of manifold sources. In the 1890s, translations of Baudelaire, Mallarmé, Verlaine, Catulle Mendès, and others were disseminated throughout the continent in magazines and journals from several cities. A wide network of readership, translation, and commentary existed, the conditions of which led to the characteristics of the *modernista*'s writing on which we have commented so far.[59] In *A. de Gilbert*, Darío relates how during his spell in Chile he had access to the latest French magazines: "en todas partes libros, libros clásicos y las últimas novedades de la producción universal, en especial la francesa. Sobre una mesa diarios, las pilas azules y rojas de la Nouvelle Revue y la Revue de Deux Mondes."[60] As a creative reader who rewrites, translates, and annotates what he reads, Darío's work reflects these *modernista* reading practices from the margins. In his writing, he inscribes the names of the authors with whom the readership of his network is familiar, thereby also inscribing their lexicon, tropes, and styles. Nevertheless, Darío's ambition is not merely to appeal to a large readership with which he shares an enthusiasm for the novelties of European (above all French) and North American poetry. More than that, he wants to be read on a par with Gautier, Banville, Verlaine, and Mendès.[61] As mentioned earlier, that also means being read from within French literary tradition, and if possible, becoming a French-language writer, as Augusto de Armas, Lautreámont, and Jean Moréas managed to do. Because being read in such a way is synonymous with becoming part of the Western Canon, Darío overtly links his poetry to all those poets who already inhabit that privileged space. Explicit mentions of Hugo, Verlaine, Banville, Gautier, etc., abound in his writing. Those names are not merely ciphers of a sensual experience with foreign signs; they are marks of prestige, erudition, and worldliness.

In the next chapter, I will analyze the pan-Latinist turn in Darío's poetry writing, after which he would add other linguistic layers to his multilingual writing. In doing so, he will traverse the tradition of Iberian literature all the way to its Latin roots.

2

Not Only from the Roses of Paris

The Pan-Latinist Turn in Darío's Writing

A shift seems to take place in Darío's writing with the second edition of *Prosas profanas* (1901), in which he expanded the collection by adding over twenty poems written during the years 1898–1901. If we follow the dates on which the poems were written, it becomes clear that after 1898 (the year of the Spanish-American war) Darío began to explore the history of Iberian literature in his poetry, first by rewriting Provençal poetry with "Dezires, layes y canciones" in the second edition of *Prosas profanas*, and then by going as far as attempting Latin hexameters in *Cantos de vida y esperanza* and *El canto errante*, in addition to incorporating Catalan into some of the poems of the latter collection.

The dates of the composition of the twenty-odd poems added to *Prosas* also coincide with Darío's trip to chronicle post-war Spain in late 1898. Critics such as Zavala see "Cosas del Cid," analyzed in Chapter 1, as the threshold between the poetry of *Prosas* and after, given its emphasis on the Spanishness of *El Cid*.[1] This shift, however, does not mean that the French echoes fade away in Darío's writing. On the contrary, in *Cantos de vida y esperanza* Darío continues to experiment with the forms and styles of French poetry, but he does so with added layers. Critics have paid due attention to the sociopolitical themes of the collection, discussing the differences of theme and style in relation to *Prosas profanas*.[2] However, the new linguistic layers that are added to Darío's writing have been scarcely discussed. For that reason, in this chapter I will focus only on the echoes of languages other than French in Darío's oeuvre after 1898.

It is a common mistake to view Darío's anti-imperialist pan-Latinism as an isolated shift of his erstwhile Francophilia. Just as the latter came about in the midst of an enthusiastic network of readers that spanned Latin America, pan-Latinism was an ideology that brought together many intellectuals and writers in the wake of both the Franco–Prussian and Spanish–American wars. Writers profoundly admired by Darío—José Martí, Gaspar Núñez de Arce, Marcelino Ménendez Pelayo, Juan Valera, Paul Groussac—were openly against US imperialism, and many of them advocated for a Latinist renewal: the cultural unity of the so-called heirs of Greco-Roman culture, which in their view comprised France, Southern Europe, and Latin America.[3]

Before analyzing the new linguistic layers, it's worth looking at an article published by Darío in the periodical *El Tiempo* of Buenos Aires in May 1898, as a way of charting the ideological shifts in his worldview. The article, titled "El triunfo de Calibán," is a response to three lectures attended by Darío on the subject of US intervention in Cuba, one of which was given summarized by Paul Groussac.

Most of the sociopolitical themes of *Cantos* are synthesized in the text: the brotherhood of France and Spain, the threat of US imperialism, the noble grandeur of Hispanic culture, and so forth. Darío anticipates the reaction of his readers, who, bearing in mind his previous criticism of Spain's cultural stagnation, might have found themselves puzzled by his sudden change of heart: "«¿Y Ud. no ha atacado siempre a España?» Jamás," he writes, before waxing apologetic:

> España no es el fanático curial, ni el pedantón, ni el dómine feliz, desdeñoso de la América que no conoce; la España que yo defiendo se llama Hidalguía, Ideal, Nobleza; se llama Cervantes, Quevedo, Góngora, Gracián, Velázquez; se llama el Cid, Loyola, Isabel; se llama la Hija de Roma, la Hermana de Francia, la Madre de América.[4]

If we read the passage closely, it becomes clear that what Spain represents for Darío is, first of all, an ideal that he associates with a literature, and second, the body of written works that constitutes that literature. The references to writers, artists, and renowned historical figures do not include anyone contemporary to Darío: they are all canonical figures of the past. If we also look at *Cantos de vida y esperanza*, neither do we find there anything about the Spain of his day. The only trace is the epigraph to "Al rey Óscar," which is taken from the French newspaper *Le Figaro*—and even so, the poem that follows the quote has a mythical setting. The Spain of *Cantos* is not so much a nation or a country as it is a literary tradition, which Darío conceives, as he says in the passage above, as a daughter of Rome and a sister of France.

This ideological shift had its poetic corollary: in addition to the French echoes analyzed in the previous chapter, Darío added echoes of Provençal, Early Modern Spanish, Catalan, and Latin. A seemingly insignificant detail in Darío's spelling serves as trace of the shift: In *Prosas profanas* Darío transposed French words into Spanish, effectively converting them into Spanish-language Gallicisms. Among these words, and at the heart of Darío's poetics, was *harmonía*, which Darío deliberately spelled with "h" to resemble the French *harmonie*. In *Cantos*, however, Darío drops the "h" and *harmonía* reverts to *armonía*. He also began to write vowels (in particular the letter "u") with a dieresis, just as Spanish poets Gonzalo de Berceo and Luis de Góngora did centuries before him. We can see this in poems such as "Helios," "Marcha triunfal," "La dulzura del Ángelus," "El verso sutil que pasa o se posa," "Nocturno," and "Ibis." He would continue to do so in his later writings. At a time when the conventions of grammar were relatively supple, the spelling of a poet obliquely reflects his vision of his language.[5]

An Exploration of Iberian Literature's Past

I will start by analyzing "Dezires, Layes y Canciones," a section that was added to *Prosas* in the second edition, in which Darío rewrites several Provençal poems in a *modernista* style. It's thanks to articles by Pedro Henríquez Ureña and José María de Cossío that we know the precise source for this series of poems: the *Cancionero inédito del siglo XV* published in Madrid in 1884 by Pérez Gómez Nieva.[6] Ureña describes it as a volume that is not well known nor should be, given the poor quality of the transcribed texts.[7] The poets of the *Cancionero* were part of the courts of Alfonso V of Aragón (also king of Naples) and John II of Castile.[8] In fifteenth-century Spain, languages such as Provençal, Galician-Portuguese, and Catalan, among others, competed with Castilian Spanish as literary languages of the Peninsula. Galician-Portuguese was hitherto traditionally used for lyric, whereas Provençal was reserved for troubadour genres. However, as the Castilian Crown expanded its rule in the Americas, so did its linguistic dominion over the Peninsula. The poets of Nieva's *Cancionero* give us a glimpse of the multilingual past of Iberian literature, which Darío inscribes into his oeuvre.

It is tempting to think that Darío did so to prove his critics wrong regarding his *afrancesamiento*, even more so if we consider José Enrique Rodó's provocative review of *Prosas profanas*. As in the poems analyzed earlier, in "Dezires, Layes y Canciones" Darío points the reader to the writers with whom he will converse. In this case, the names of the authors are at the beginning of each poem: Johan de Duenyas, Johan de Torres, Valtierra, and Santa Ffe. Darío adheres to the meter, rhyme scheme, and terminology of the poetic forms he takes from these poets (that is, "dezir," "lay," "tornada," "ffin," and so forth), suggesting that he wants to show the reader that he is renewing old forms. This archaism also includes the spelling of the poets' names, as Darío adheres to their Provençal orthography (i.e., he writes Duenyas and not Dueñas).

In keeping a similar kind of meter and rhyme scheme, Darío manages to bear over echoes of troubadour poetry by rendering the playful rhymes of nine-syllable lines and shorter. He empties the molds of these late medieval forms and fills them with *modernista* verse. Ureña describes it as follows: "¿Qué tomó Darío de aquellos poetas menores? Apenas la versificación, y, de tarde en tarde, vagas *resonancias* de estilo,—las que suelen acompañar a toda forma métrica."[9]

Among these poems his versions of Santa Ffe stand out for their quality. In "Que el amor no admite cuerdas reflexiones," Darío rewrites Santa Ffe's poem while preserving echoes of his rhymes. Below are the two initial stanzas of the poems; Darío's version is on the right.

Senyora, magüer *consiento*
E quiero sofrir mi danyo,
Mas pensat por *sentimiento*
No me 'nganyo.

Senyora, si penedir
A todos bien pareçiese,
Hora es que 'l buen serbir
En ta bos lo defendiese.
Por çelar lo que en bos *siento*

Señora, Amor es *violento*;
y cuando nos transfigura
nos enciende el *pensamiento*
la locura.

No pidas paz a mis brazos,
que a los tuyos tienen presos;
son de guerra mis abrazos
y son de incendio mis besos;
y sería vano *intento*

Ensuenyo que no me 'nsanyo,	el tornar mi mente obscura,
Más pensat por *sentimiento*	si me enciende el *pensamiento*
No me 'nganyo. (ll. 1–12)	la locura. (ll. 1–12)

As with the previous poems, I have emphasized the words that are resonant in both texts. On the one hand, Darío is rewriting Provençal poetry into modern Spanish. On the other, he not only starts his poem in the same way as his source, but he constructs his rhymes with words that echo those of Santa Ffe. As a result, Santa Ffe's poem is improved upon in Darío's, who has heightened its rhythm through the sibilant alliteration of lines 5–8, which intensify the trope of love as war, and build on the tension of the poem's theme which has suddenly become that of love dogged by madness.

His other version of Santa Ffe, "Copla Esparça," could be placed alongside "Cosas del Cid," "A maestre Gonzalo de Berceo," and "Cyrano en España" as poems in which Spain and France appear shoulder to shoulder as harmonious counterparts in a pan-Latinist manner.[10] These are texts in which Darío's intent to bridge two traditions (French and Hispanic) is rendered visible. Also, it's worth adding that Provençal poetry is something that both French and Hispanic literary traditions share historically, which makes Darío's choice of these poems more significant. In "Copla Esparça," Darío's ever-evolving poetics is crystallized in a sonnet that makes Verlaine fit within a Provençal poem.

In this *modernista* version, the original title is archaistic and remains unchanged, as does overall the structure of the poem (eight lines plus four for the "Tornada"). Darío preserves the metrical scheme present in Santa Ffe, whose stanzas for the most part combine octosyllable lines with a final tetrasyllabic one. This makes the rhythm of his poem like that of its Provençal counterpart. However, while Santa Ffe's "Copla" sings the praises of a woman envied by others for her character and beauty, Darío's is an erotic description of a lover in the nude. It starts with an allusion to Verlaine's "Femme et chatte" from *Poèmes saturniens* (1866). In Verlaine's poem, woman and cat mirror each other and exchange traits: as the woman is rendered feline, the cat becomes feminine. This sleight of hand is achieved through a chiaroscuro: the whiteness of the womanly hand and the feline paw contrast with the shadows surrounding them:

> Elle jouait avec sa chatte,
> Et c'était merveille de voir
> La main blanche et la blanche patte
> S'ébattre dans l'ombre du soir. (ll. 1–4)

How does this make its way into Darío's poem?

> ¡La gata blanca! En el lecho
> maya, se encorva, se extiende.
> Un rojo rubí se enciende
> sobre los globos del pecho. (ll. 1–4)

Darío forgoes the subtlety of Verlaine's play of light and shade to directly describe the woman as a cat crouching and stretching on the bed. He then describes the black tresses over her breasts using what will become one of the central symbols of *Cantos*, the swan:

> Los desatados cabellos
> la divina espalda aroman.
> Bajo la camisa asoman
> dos cisnes de negros cuellos. (ll. 5–8)

By contrast, Santa Ffe is moralistic:

> Tanto, senyora, baledes,
> Que las damas birtuosas,
> Biben de bos rezelosas
> Que la fama les robedes.
> A toda mujer que bal
> Si se plaz haçer buen hecho,
> Para non errar el trecho
> Tome á bos por senyal. (ll. 1–8)

In what amounts to a new chapter for *Modernismo*'s project of metrical renewal, Darío empties Santa Ffe's poem of its content to make use of its Provençal mold. The result is a version of Verlaine's "Femme et chatte" in which ardent eroticism takes the place of umbrageous seduction and in which symbolist poetry meets troubadour verse.

In general, the added poems of 1901 are written in such a way that Darío the reader is indistinguishable from Darío the writer. If names such as Hugo, Verlaine, Banville, and Gautier crowded the lines of the previous poems, now we also find names such as Quevedo, Berceo, Anacreon, and Ovid. For instance, here is the first stanza of "A los poetas risueños":

> Anacreonte, padre de la sana alegría;
> Ovidio, sacerdote de la ciencia amorosa;
> Quevedo, en cuyo cáliz licor jovial rebosa;
> Banville, insigne orfeo de la sacra Harmonía; (ll. 1–4)

And from "A maestre Gonzalo de Berceo,"

> Amo tu delicioso alejandrino
> como el de Hugo, espíritu de España;
> éste vale una copa de champaña,
> como aquél vale «un vaso de bon vino». (ll. 1–4)

In which Darío is directly quoting from Berceo's *Vida de Santo Domingo de Silos* (1240),

> Quiero fer una prosa en román paladino,
> En qual suele ël pueblo fablar a su vecino,
> Ca non so tan letrado por fer otro latino.
> Bien valdrá, commo creo, *un vaso de bon vino*. (ll. 5–8; emphasis added)

Darío's exploration of the peninsula's past does not stop here. In the poetic sequence "Trébol," he imbues his writing with echoes of early modern Spanish. The poem, a triple sonnet, could be divided into two sections: the first, comprised of the first two sonnets, is an imagined dialogue between seventeenth-century Spanish poet Luis de Góngora y Argote and painter Diego Velázquez. In the second section, comprising the third sonnet, the speaker (ostensibly Darío himself) addresses both Góngora and Velázquez to sing their praises.

The setting itself is worth commenting, as many of the poems of *Cantos* are dialogic pieces. Most of the time the speaker either directly addresses the addressee of his poem or is staged in a dialogue with them. In "Al Rey Óscar," he addresses the king directly:

> Así, Sire, en el aire de la Francia nos llega (l. 1);

In "Salutación a Leonardo":
> Maestro: Pomona levanta tu cesto […] (l. 1);

In "A Roosevelt":
> Es con voz de la Biblia, o verso de Walt Whitman
> que habría de llegar hasta ti, Cazador (ll. 1–2);

In "«Spes»":
> Jesús, incomparable perdonador de injurias,
> óyeme […]' (ll. 1–2);

In "Melancolía":
> Hermano, tú que tienes la luz, dime la mía (l. 1)

It's a natural evolution from the kind of allusions analyzed in the previous chapter, in which the names of prestigious European writers are inscribed into the poems themselves. Gradually, those names become part of the writing. In the case of "Trébol," it's easy to see how the fantasy of a reader takes the shape of a poem: to imagine a dialogue between two admired artists and to speak to them. In doing so, the names of Góngora and Velázquez also become inscribed into the work.

According to Marasso, the models for the poem can be found in two of Cervantes's works: *Don Quijote* (1605) and *Viaje del Parnaso* (1614).[11] After rereading both works side by side with Darío's poem, only a presence of the former seems clear. In the case of the *Quijote*, Darío uses the sonnets from the "Versos preliminaries" at the beginning of the novel, where we find titles similar to the poem's "De Don Luis de Góngora y Argote a Don Diego de Silva Velázquez," such as "De Solisdán a don Quijote de la Mancha" or "Orlando furioso a don Quijote de la Mancha." The similarities are so plain that if we would replace the names of Góngora and Velázquez with those of the Amadís or Orlando, Darío's poem would easily fit in that section of Cervantes's novel with, however, a key difference: Cervantes is parodic while Darío is eulogizing. Marasso identifies parallelisms between the second section of Darío's poem and another of the sonnets of the *Quijote* found later in the novel.[12] Below, Cervantes's sestet is on the left and Darío's on the right.

> Y si de su Amadís se precia Gaula,　　　A Teócrito y Poussin la Fama dote
> por cuyos bravos descendientes Grecia　　con la corona del laurel supremo;

triunfó mil veces, y su fama ensancha,	que en donde da Cervantes el Quijote
hoy a Quijote le corona el aula do Belona preside, y dél se precia	y yo las telas con mis luces gemo, para Don Luis de Góngora y Argote
más que Grecia, ni Gaula, la alta Mancha,	traerá una nueva palma Polifemo.

If we strip the poems of their different contexts, the content of the sonnets is similar. In Darío's sonnet the message is that Góngora will also achieve fame, just as Cervantes, Velázquez, Theocritus, and Poussin did.[13] Whereas in the Cervantine sonnet, the message is that don Quijote, just as the Amadís did in Gaula, will also achieve fame in La Mancha. When read side by side, the tone is also similar; nevertheless, Darío is not quite rewriting Cervantes as he did Gautier or Banville. The fact that the *modernista* reverts Cervantes's parody in his eulogy points to an entirely different use of the source text which is far from the *aemulatio* of his French counterparts. Rather than dialoguing with Cervantes, Darío seems to inscribe him into his work. Still, the poem shares enough traits with the Spaniard's as to make it seem written according to the Cervantine sonnet.

What's more, Cervantes and his *Quijote* are explicitly mentioned in the poem, a gesture that is never gratuitous in Darío. In line 8 of the second sonnet, Darío alludes to *Angélica* and *Medoro*, characters both of Ariosto's *Orlando furioso*—an allusion which puts us squarely in the world of *don Quijote*—and Góngora's *Romance de Angélica y Medoro*.[14] Darío underlines points of contact between his writers. The third sonnet also has elements of Ariosto. In line 2 the speaker mentions a hippogriff, the mythological creature that the *Orlando* made famous: "y vela tu hipogrifo, Velázquez, la Fortuna" (l. 2). Later on, in a typically Cervantine gesture, Darío makes Ariosto's *Angélica* meet Velázquez's *Meninas*: "y mientras pasa Angélica sonriendo a las Meninas" (l. 13). The effect of Ariosto's presence in the poem is twofold: on the one hand, it engages with the characters and motifs of early modern Spanish literature; on the other, it coheres with the poem's setting: seventeenth-century Spain, the Spain of both Góngora and Velázquez. The poem showcases turns of phrase and a vocabulary which are deliberately taken from Early Modern Spanish. In the first sonnet we find:

diamante parangón de la pintura (l. 4);
Yo en equívoco altar, tú en sacro fuego (l. 9);
con la alma luz, de tu pincel el juego
el alma duplicó de la faz mía (ll. 13–14).

In the second:

a preludiar el himno a tu decoro (l. 4);
y yo las telas con mis luces gemo (l. 12).

Lastly, in the third, there is a Gongorine allusion in italics:

En tanto *pace estrellas* el Pegaso divino (l. 1)

And finally:

Gloriosa la península que abriga tal colonia (l. 9).

Octavio Paz is one of the few commentators to have identified this:

> Plenitud verbal, lo mismo en los poemas libres que en esas admirables recreaciones de la retórica barroca que son los sonetos de *Trébol*; soltura, fluidez, sorpresa continua de un lenguaje en perpetuo movimiento.[15]

These are not only subtle echoes of Góngora and Cervantes, but, more generally, of past moments in the history of the Spanish language. It's a project of poetic revival. Darío explicitly mentions this in "Historia de mis libros":

> Al escribir Cantos de vida y esperanza, yo había explorado no solamente el campo de poéticas extranjeras, sino también los cancioneros antiguos, la obra ya completa, ya fragmentaria, de los primitivos de la poesía española, en los cuales encontré riqueza de expresión y de gracia que en vano se buscarán en harto celebrados autores de siglos más cercanos.[16]

The presence of the *Quijote* in *Cantos* can hardly be overstated; it's alluded to in at least seven poems: "Cyrano en España," "XI," "Helios," "Los Cisnes I," "Trébol," "Un soneto a Cervantes," and "Letanía de nuestro señor Don Quijote." Sometimes in surprisingly inventive ways, such as in these lines from "Helios":

que del alma-Quijote y el cuerpo-Sancho Panza
vuele una psique cierta a la verdad del sueño (ll. 53–4).

This does not imply that Darío was discovering the writers mentioned above. Rather, by espousing French and Hispanic traditions on the one hand, and probing the history of Iberian literature on the other, Darío brought to life again not only Spanish but Greco-Roman classics.

At the turn of the century, this exploration of the literatures of the past was in the air. As Pérez Priego explains, the interest on the part of the Pre-Raphaelites in reviving medieval art and literature was part of a larger trend to revive forgotten or canonical works of the past.[17] In this regard, Darío was also likely inspired by Jean Moréas's *L'école romane*, a movement that rejected Symbolism's alleged obscurity in favor of a neo-classicist revival of Greco-Roman poetry. Darío admired Moréas and praised him in *Los raros*. If one reads Moréas's *Les Stances* (1893) side by side with Darío's shorter poems of *Cantos* ("«Spes»," "Filosofía," "De otoño," "Amo, amas…, " "Ibis," and "Thanatos") their similarities become clear: they are short, four- to eight-line long, wistful poems, often with a rhyme scheme of ABAB written in a straightforward and heartfelt manner. Unfortunately, critics have limited their reading of *Cantos* by and large to the context of pan-Hispanism. If, however, we take the influence of *L'école romane* on the one hand, and that of the poetry of Virgil, Horace, and Ovid on the other, the presence of Latin literature in Darío's writing of the time comes to the fore.

Darío's writing gradually incorporated interlocutors from past and present, both fictional and historical, evolving toward a more capacious discourse that went beyond French literature and involved Classical authors as well. Not surprisingly Sylvia Molloy has defined his poetry as being animated by two binary movements: "Voracidad y solipsismo. Por un lado, la necesidad de penetrar y de incorporar: por el otro, la necesidad de cerrarse, de no dejarse incorporar."[18] To elaborate on Molloy's point, what we find in Darío is, on the one hand, a voracity for culture, women, and languages, and, on the other, what Molloy calls solipsism (surely in a figurative sense) since the speaker of these poems absorbs and increasingly incorporates the names and styles of others, making them his own. Darío's writing becomes increasingly self-referential. With this I do not mean that Darío reflects on his life through his poems, which is a truism; rather, that in certain poems the speaker explicitly reflects on the characteristics of his own poetry, in a sort of internal allusion or intratextuality, such as in "Yo soy aquel …" from *Cantos de vida y esperanza* or "Epístola" from *El canto errante*.

This shift toward the history of Iberian literature and the Classics coincided not only with Moréas's *L'école romane*, but with the end of *Symbolisme*, which according to Schmigalle left a void for the Nicaraguan poet that the emergent avant-gardes would never come to fill.[19]

Darío's Latinate Writings

Other classics of Western literature appear alongside Cervantes, among which the most noteworthy are Ovid, Dante, the authors of the Bible, and Virgil. Ovid, who was already alluded to in the second edition of *Prosas*, makes his appearance in the poems "Los Cisnes" and "Ibis."[20] In the former, Darío writes,

> Yo te saludo ahora como en versos latinos
> te saludara antaño Publio Ovidio Nasón.
> Los mismos ruiseñores cantan los mismos trinos,
> y en diferentes lenguas es la misma canción.
> A vosotros mi lengua no debe ser extraña.
> A Garcilaso visteis, acaso, alguna vez … (ll. 5–10)

The fragment is revealing because Darío again puts forth a lineage. The swans, mysterious symbols of a higher power, are the privileged audience of some of the great poets of history: Ovid, Garcilaso, and now Darío. On the other hand, what stands out is the unity of this lineage beyond linguistic differences, which is part and parcel of Darío's understanding of literature (mentioned in Chapter 1) as something that transcends both national and linguistic boundaries.

"Ibis," the other poem in which Ovid is openly mentioned, is also noteworthy. In four lines—a Moréan poem—Darío plays with the double meaning of the word which is at once the title of Ovid's well-known poem of exile as well as the name of a bird:

> Cuidadoso estoy siempre ante el Ibis de Ovidio,
> enigma humano tan ponzoñoso y süave

que casi no pretende su condición de ave
cuando se ha conquistado sus terrores de ofidio. (ll. 1–4)

The pun suggests that, by force of its venom, Ovid's bitter poem is closer to a snake than to a bird. What makes this minor piece of *Cantos* noteworthy is that it takes us directly to Darío the reader—it seems as if it were jotted down on the margins of his edition of *Ibis*. If we read closely, we see the poem begins in line 1 by relating the act of reading.[21]

So far I have analyzed poems that show how the writing of Darío is imbued with echoes of French and other moments of Spanish and Provençal, in addition to its references to Ovid. However, Darío attempted to have another language wrought into his writing: Latin. Before looking at his attempt to write in hexameters, it must be said that Latin phrases abound in all Darío's oeuvre—a trait that became more pervasive in his later work. We find them both as titles and as lines made to rhyme with Spanish, as Darío also occasionally does with Italian and English.[22] This is yet another aspect of the multilingualism of Darío's oeuvre. "Madrigal exaltado," for example, begins as follows:

Dies irae, dies illa!
Solvet saeclum in favilla
cuando quema esa pupila! (ll. 1–3)

Darío uses the verses from the well-known Latin hymn to begin his single-rhymed triplets, rhyming the two Latin words with a Spanish one: *illa, favilla, pupila*. Similarly, in "Yo soy aquel ... ":

Vida, luz y verdad, tal triple llama
produce la interior llama infinita;
el Arte puro como Cristo exclama:
Ego sum lux et veritas et vita! (ll. 85–8)

Here he tampers with the vulgate passage "Ego sum via, veritas et vita" (*Latin Vulgate*, John 14:6) by changing it for his own purposes, both so it can fit the meter of his stanza and it can rhyme with *infinita*, drawing a parallelism with the *vida, luz y verdad* of line 85. Here is another example from a poem analyzed earlier, "Que el amor no admite cuerdas reflexiones":

> Mi gozo tu paladar
> rico panal conceptúa,
> como en el santo Cantar:
> *Mel et lac sub lingua tua.* (ll. 21–4)

Darío resorts to the baroque *conceptúa* to complete the rhyme with the line taken from the *Song of Songs*. Other examples include poems that have a Latin word as title, such as "«Spes»" and "«Charitas»" from *Cantos*. Hugo's work is similarly ripe with Latin dicta and words, many of them from the Bible. Osvaldo Bazil, a Dominican writer and close friend of Darío, describes the poet's relation to languages other than Spanish as follows:

> No tuvo [Darío] facilidad para aprender idiomas. No habló ni escribió bien ningún idioma extranjero. Se defendía nada más que regularmente con su rudimentario conocimiento del francés, del inglés, del latín y del italiano. El que mejor leía era el francés. Después de veinte años de vivir en París y leer clásicos y modernos franceses, no pudo adquirir el acento parisiense ni soltura al hablarlo […] Leía la Biblia. Era casi su libro único y su única lectura en muchos años. En todos los países donde llegaba, Rubén adquiría un ejemplar de la Biblia. Exigía que fuera con el texto en latín, con la traducción española al frente. Él no hablaba ni leía latín, pero lo entendía un poco y le gustaba citar el texto en latín en sus escritos.[23]

The text is surprising for presenting a Darío who, despite his love for and vast culture of French language and literature, could never master the language.[24] Also, Bazil shows that Darío strove to incorporate Latin into his writing, in a manner that corroborates what I have mentioned thus far. This was common practice among French writers from Voltaire to Hugo; in Darío's case, the practice seems to have increased after 1898 and would remain constant until his death.

There are seven poems in *Cantos* in which either the title or a line is in Latin. One could find other examples in his prose and in his earlier poetry collections. However, what sets *Cantos* apart as far as Latin goes is Darío's assertion of having achieved Latin hexameters in Spanish. In the preface he says the following:

> En todos los países cultos de Europa se ha usado el hexámetro absolutamente clásico, sin que la mayoría letrada y, sobre todo, la minoría leída, se

asustasen de semejante manera de cantar. En Italia ha mucho tiempo, sin citar antiguos, que Carducci ha autorizado los hexámetros; en inglés, no me atrevería casi a indicar, por respeto a la cultura de mis lectores, que la *Evangelina*, de Longfellow, está en los mismos versos en que Horacio dijo sus mejores pensares.[25]

In "Historia de mis libros" he expands on the point through what often seems like pan-Hispanist rhetoric:

Español de América y americano de España, canté, eligiendo como instrumento el hexámetro griego y latino, mi confianza y mi fe en el renacimiento de la vieja Hispania en el propio solar y del otro lado del Océano, en el coro de naciones que hacen contrapeso en la balanza sentimental a la fuerte y osada raza del Norte. Elegí el hexámetro por ser de tradición grecolatina y porque yo creo, después de haber estudiado el asunto, que en nuestro idioma, malgré [sic] la opinión de tantos catedráticos, hay sílabas largas y breves, y que lo que ha faltado es un análisis más hondo y musical de nuestra prosodia. Un buen lector ha de advertir en seguida los correspondientes valores, y lo que han hecho Voss y otros en alemán, Longfellow y tantos en inglés, Carducci, D'Annunzio y otros en Italia, Villegas, el P. Martín y Eusebio Caro, el colombiano, y todos los que cita Eugenio Melé en su trabajo sobre la Poesía bárbara en España, bien podíamos continuarlo otros, aristocratizando así nuevos pensares.[26]

In the latter passage we can see how Darío explicitly presents his hexameters as a cultural project within the Latinist renewal of which he feels part. How successful is Darío in transposing hexameters into Spanish? In *Los hexámetros castellanos y en particular los de Rubén Darío* (1935), Julio Saavedra Molina points out that Darío's knowledge of hexameters was lacking, especially when, as in the passage above, he does not distinguish between Voss and Carducci's hexameters, two authors who followed distinct methods.[27] Voss's hexameter is a strict six-foot line which is spondaic (a spondee is a foot made of two syllables both stressed or long). Other German writers, such as Goethe or Klopstock, favored trochaic hexameters instead of Voss's spondaic ones; that is, lines in which the foot has one long or stressed syllable followed by one short or weak syllable. For all these writers, however, a foot can only be two or maximum three syllables long, but not more than that.[28] By contrast, the rules of Carducci's hexameters are laxer: The unit of the foot is no longer restricted to two or three syllables. In Carducci's version there is almost no concern for the length of a foot; the focus seems only to be on writing lines made of six stresses or six long syllables. Though this sometimes leads to lines that do work as hexameters, the method permits so much variety that the overall meter of the poem often ends up being altogether different. In some poems, we can find lines of five or seven stresses with feet five-syllables-long.[29] Needless to say, they are not hexameters.

After a close analysis of "Salutación del optimista," Saavedra points out that Darío clearly tried to follow the laxer method, albeit with dubious success.[30] Nonetheless, of the fifty-nine lines of the poem, at least thirteen are proper hexameters in the sense in which writers such as Goethe or Klopstock thought of. Here are some examples:

> Ínclitas / razas u/bérrimas, / sangre de His/pania fe/cunda, [...] (l. 1)
> Mágicas / ondas de / vida / van rena/ciendo de / pronto; [...] (l. 5)
> tiene su / coro de / vástagos, / altos ro/bustos y / fuertes. [...] (l. 37)
> Sangre de His/pania fec/unda, / sólidas / ínclitas / razas [...] (l. 40)
> Juntas las / testas an/cianas, ce/ñidas de / líricos / lauros (l. 44)

I have scanned the lines to emphasize the six stresses where the feet are no more than three syllables long. When read aloud, the distinct rhythm of the lines should ring clear even to those unfamiliar with Latin prosody. Although the poem is not written in hexameters proper, lines like these carry echoes of the Latin meter. Moreover, some of the words Darío uses are deliberately redolent of Latin, as he often employs Latinate diction: for example, *Hispania* is the Roman name for present-day Spain, and ¡*salve!* is a salutation that comes directly from the Latin *salve*. He uses *testas* from the Latin *testa* instead of *cabezas*; *súbito* from *subitus*; *ínclita* from *inclitus*; *ubérrimo* from *uberrimus*; and so forth. Also, in a typically Darian gesture, he openly alludes to Virgil in the poem:

> y en la caja pandórica de que tantas desgracias surgieron
> encontramos de súbito, talismánica, pura, riente,
> cual pudiera decirla en sus versos Virgilio divino,
> la divina reina de luz, ¡la celeste Esperanza! (ll. 7–10)

As mentioned earlier, this is never gratuitous when it comes to Darío's poetry. Marasso finds correspondences between some of the lines of the poem and Virgil's fourth Eclogue.[31] The line se anuncia un reino Nuevo, feliz sibila sueña (l. 7) is resonant of Virgil's Ultima Cumaei venit iam carminis aetas; Magnus ab integro saeclorum nascitur ordo (ll. 5–6) which in Eugenio de Ochoa's translation, the version to which Darío most likely had access, appears as: "ya llega la última edad enunciada en los versos de la Sibila de Cumas."[32]

The hexameter would remain a form of interest for Darío in *El canto errante*. It's the putative meter in which he wrote his controversial "Salutación al Águila"[33]—a poem which critics have read narrowly for the ideological contradiction it supposes, overlooking its form and meter—and "«In memoriam» Bartolomé Mitre."[34] And as far as his use of Latin goes, all of Darío's major poems thereafter would include at least a phrase or dictum: "Epístola," "Poema del otoño," "Canto a la Argentina," "La Cartuja," even the French poem "«France-Amérique»" discussed earlier.[35] The ending of "«In memoriam» Bartolomé Mitre" explicitly sums up what we have so far pointed out: both the addition of a new linguistic layer that comes from Classics such as Horace and Virgil, as well as the incorporation of new poetic meters such as the attempted hexameter:

> Yo, que de la argentina tierra siento el influjo en mi mente,
> «llevo mi palma y canto a la fiesta del gran argentino»,
> recordando el hexámetro que vibraba en la lira de Horacio,
> y a Virgilio latino, guía excelso y amado del Dante.[36] (ll. 33–6)

Bringing It All Together: Darío's Use of Catalan

In the course of his wandering life, Darío sojourned twice in Mallorca, seeking peace and quiet from his fraught Parisian life: first in the winter of 1906–07 and then in 1913. Despite spanning only months at a time, they were prolific periods: most of his poetic and fictional writings after 1905 are a result of his time spent in the Balearic Island. There he wrote many of the poems that comprise *El canto errante* and *El canto a la Argentina y otros poemas*, as well as the two unfinished novels: *La isla de oro* and *El oro de Mallorca*.³⁷ During his first sojourn, he wrote two poems that use Catalan sparsely though inventively, both later collected in *El canto errante*. One of these, "Epístola," is one of the most important poems in Darío's oeuvre.

As I have pointed out elsewhere, it's Darío's great poem of Parisian disillusion.³⁸ It has mostly been read as an autobiographical document and a precursor of the ironic and colloquial turn that would take place in Spanish American poetry. However, what has been overlooked is that in this poem Darío's multilingual poetics finally crystallizes and comes together more fully—pointing, perhaps, to the kind of poetry he would have written had he lived longer and continued to develop his writing.

Bursting with irony and self-mockery, the poem is written in a Spanish that at times mixes French, Latin, and Catalan, finding novel and original rhymes in the words of these languages which often end on flat, sardonic monosyllables set in couplets—a long way from the preciosity of *Prosas profanas* and the heartfelt manner of *Cantos de vida y esperanza*. It's also a poem of travel: the speaker travels, and the voyage from one city to another is related in the poem itself, so that Darío's errant life becomes palpable in its unfolding: From Antwerp to Buenos Aires (and in between a stint in Rio de Janeiro), from the River Plate to Paris, and from there on to Mallorca, the location where the poem ends.

The language played with changes according to geography. Thus, the text begins in French because the speaker finds himself in Antwerp, ostensibly writing a letter to someone in Argentina (hence the title of the poem):

Madame Lugones, j'ai commencé ces vers
en écoutant la voix d'un carillon d'Anvers …
Así empecé, en francés, pensando en Rodenbach,
cuando hice hacia el Brasil una fuga … ¡de Bach! (ll. 1–4)

The speaker breaks into Spanish to comment on the beginning of his own poem, which he says to have written in French thinking of Belgian Symbolist Georges Rodenbach. In the fourth line he mentions his small escapade (*una fuga*) to Brazil, but ends the line punning on the word *fuga*, which means both an escape and a musical composition, with a non sequitur in allusion to Johann Sebastian Bach. In stark contrast to his previous poetry, the lines are brashly out of kilter.

Further on, in an allusion to Virgil's *Eclogae*, Darío uses Latin to have it rhyme with Spanish: "Mi ditirambo brasileño es ditirambo/que aprobaría tu marido. Arcades ambo." (ll. 21–2).[39] The *marido* here refers to the addressee's husband and Darío's protégé, Leopoldo Lugones, pointing to how he would approve these lines whose style seem so like his own. Indeed, the tone that pervades "Epístola" is strikingly similar to that of the Lugones of *Los crepúsculos del jardín* (1905), which was published a year before this poem was written, particularly those poems that comprise the second half of the collection, such as "El solterón," "Melancolía," and "Los cuatro amores de Dryopos." In fact, the two latter poems are written in the same meter and rhyme scheme as "Epístola."[40]

Otherwise, the Spanish poem brims with moments of French—it includes nine phrases in French and at least two additional Gallicisms in translation, with some particularly inventive rhymes such as:

> Es preciso que el médico que eso recete, dé
> también libro de cheques para el *Crédit Lyonnais* (ll. 47–8)

Or:

> [...] Y me volví a París. Me volví al enemigo
> terrible, centro de la neurosis, ombligo
> de la locura, foco de todo *surmenage*
> donde hago buenamente mi papel de *sauvage*
> encerrado en mi celda de la *rue Marivaux*,
> confiando sólo en mí y resguardando el yo. (ll. 63–8)

Until the speaker arrives in Mallorca. Darío then uses some Catalan:

> Hoy, heme aquí en Mallorca, *la terra dels foners*
> como dice Mossen Cinto, el gran Catalán [...]
> Y saludan con un *bon dia tengui* gracioso,
> entre los cestos llenos de patatas y coles. (ll. 98–9; 124–5)

While the instances of Catalan are merely the two above, they appear alongside a playful description of the speaker's residence in the island, the town's marketplace, and his admiration for Ramón Llul. Darío engages with the cultural history of Mallorca the island, and in addition to Llul, mentions Santiago Rusiñol, George Sand, and Frédéric Chopin, as well as several important locations. He inscribes language and geography into his poem, so that the text reflects the changing landscapes which surround its author. Darío also used Catalan in another poem of *El canto errante*, "Agencia," again ironically:

> En la iglesia el diablo se esconde.
> Ha parido una monja ... (¿En dónde?) ...
> Barcelona ya no está *bona*
> sino cuando la bomba *sona* ... (ll. 13–16)

The poem is a sarcastic listing of all things that have gone awry in the world, and in the two lines above Darío puns on the Catalan proverb "Barcelona és bona si la bossa sona," referring to the high prices of the city, to comment on recent explosions carried out by local anarchist groups.

Yet Mallorca in particular, and his engagement with Catalan intellectual life through Gabriel Alomar and Santiago Rusiñol, brought about a greater change in Darío's writing. As can be seen in the poems written during that winter, he greatly simplified the language of his poetry, rendering it more conversational and ironic. Alongside his style, his themes also changed; besides exploring the notion of metempsychosis, his poems looked increasingly toward nature, reading in the shapes of its creatures and the patterns of its landscapes either the messages of a higher plane of existence or the prophecy of a Second Coming. Self-interrogation became pervasive. New landscapes arose: the island of Mallorca became the privileged setting of many writings, and its Mediterranean location made Darío feel even more deeply connected to the tradition of Latin literature.

"Epístola" is unique within Darío's oeuvre, among other things because it reveals the dark underbelly of cosmopolitanism. If we compare the picture of a life of travels found there with that of "Divagación" or even "Yo soy aquél," the contrast is impossible to ignore. Throughout its more than 200 lines, Darío consistently subverts the ideas he previously upheld as the hero of *Modernismo*—Paris as the city of dreams; the importance of the political destiny of Spanish America; poetry as a higher form of truth in a capitalist world, etc. The fact that several languages in the poem correspond with the speaker's vagrant itinerary is a natural evolution of Darío's multilingual poetics, which sought to broaden the cultural landscapes of its writing by crossing the linguistic borders that often separate literatures, to absorb them and make them his own. Though ignored by critics, it's a thread that runs through all the Nicaraguan's oeuvre, as is clear if we look at the early poem "La poesía castellana," dated 1882 in San Salvador, when Darío was about fifteen years old.[41]

As its title suggests, the poem is an overview of the history of Spanish poetry in which the changes the Spanish language underwent are enacted in the poem itself: It begins by discussing *El Cid* in the language of *El Cid*, and chronicles linguistic history by doing the same with Alfonso *El Sabio*, Santillana, the Golden Age, and eventually ending with the Spanish Americans Ricardo Palma and Ricardo Marroquín—all the while imitating their respective styles. Below are the first six lines, which start with *El Cid*:

> Fablávase rvda et torpe fabla
> cuando vevía grand Cid Campeador,
> e lvego quando le fiçieron trovas,
> ben sopieron trovas le far.
> A guisa de regocixo ponyanse a trovar
> e cantábanl'a las dueinas con polido cantar. (ll. 1–6)

Darío includes archaic spelling and syntax. As the poem unfolds, we see how Spanish changes from epoch to epoch and from writer to writer. After Alphonso, Johan de Mena, and Santillana appear, Spanish acquires sudden grace and beauty with Manrique according to the young Darío:

> Manrique, con galanura,
> brinda su trova fermosa
> tan sonora,
> que llena de grand finura,
> es cual la canción graciosa
> que hay agora. (ll. 51–6)

> [...] Levanta el ánimo muerto,
> recrea el ánimo vivo
> la su armonía;
> nos saca de desconcierto,
> ca tiene vigor activo,
> Philosophía. (ll. 69–74)

The spelling is closer now to modern Spanish, even more so when the speaker mentions Lope, Quevedo, Góngora, and Calderón, in a style that imitates the rhetoric of the *siglo de oro*—all preliminary work for his later poem "Trébol."

Darío ends the poem by arriving at modern Spanish with allusions to poets from "El Nuevo Mundo," effectively suggesting that the future of literature in Spanish lay in the Americas:

> Hoy resuenan por doquier
> melodías de Andrés Bello,
> dando luz con su destello
> y enseñando con su ser;
> nos sentimos conmover
> de Olmedo al *Canto de Junín,*
> y hoy admiramos, en fin,
> el genio vivo y preclaro
> de los Heredias, los Caro,
> los Palma y los Marroquín. (ll. 271–80)

Coming full circle, as it were, we can now see that Darío's multilingual streak was present in his early writing in a somewhat spectacular manner, given the poem's date of composition and its author's age. The way he studiously engaged with his sources, not only imitating but also emulating and making them his own, in the classical sense of these terms, was already there. Afterward, as we have seen, through his exploration of Spanish's past, his repurposing of Provençal forms, his attempted hexameters, his rewriting of classical sources, his constant insertion of Latin into his writing, and his sparse use of Catalan, Darío added new multilingual echoes to his poetry.

Part Two

Darío in Translation

3

English Translations of Rubén Darío

In an article published in *The Nation* in 2006, Roberto González Echevarría laments the scarce knowledge that countries beyond the Hispanic world have of the writings of Rubén Darío and Garcilaso de la Vega, arguably the two most influential poets in the history of the Spanish language. "They have not traveled well," he writes, "particularly in English-speaking countries, where they are all but unknown." He then relates why, in his opinion, this is even more surprising in the case of Darío:

> Darío's case is the most baffling because he is nearly our contemporary, whereas Garcilaso, who lived from 1501 to 1536, can today be safely left on library shelves along with Petrarch, Ronsard and Spenser. Besides, Garcilaso has by now been so thoroughly assimilated into Spanish poetic discourse that it is easy to overlook his presence in the poetry of Neruda and Paz. Darío's innovations, style and even manner are still contemporary, however, as are the polemics that his poetry provoked among other poets, professors and critics.

González Echevarría gives an overview of Darío's life and writings, showing the extent of the Nicaraguan author's influence while unpacking the context in which his work appeared. He does this to set the scene for his review of *Rubén Darío: Selected Writings* (2006), edited by Ilan Stavans and published by Penguin, which he criticizes as follows:

> Darío's circulation and reputation in English will not be helped by the publication of this carelessly conceived and executed anthology of his prose and verse. [...] The subdivisions draw their headings from the lines of a poem whose translation is particularly appalling. Greg Simon and Steven White's poetry translations are not only awkward; they make basic errors that are beyond the usual disputes about word choice.

The outrage that transpires from González Echevarría's article is telling of two gaps that stand out when we look at the reception of Darío: on the one hand, the gap between Darío's canonical status in Spanish and his obscure status in English; on the other, the gap between the high quality of Darío's writing in Spanish and the low quality of the translations in English. González Echevarría continues his article in the manner of the passage above, bemoaning the mistranslations found in the first Penguin edition of Rubén Darío.

Unfortunately, he does not tell us why Darío is all but unknown in English-speaking countries. One reason seems to be the quality of the translations, but González Echevarría never explicitly says this, perhaps because a complex array of historical, cultural, and literary factors come into play when explaining Darío's obscurity in countries not Hispanic. Answering the question requires tracing the shifting location of Spanish American literature in English, which was almost nonexistent before the 1960s and the so-called "Boom." It also raises questions regarding the reception of authors in literary cultures other than their own. Lastly, Darío's own canonical status within Spanish (which today seems beyond doubt) has changed over the past century, which is also likely to have impacted on his reception.

Darío vis-à-vis the Translation of Spanish American Literature

The "Boom" of Spanish American literature translated into English, which came to prominence in the 1960s and 1970s—and found its culmination in Gregory Rabassa's 1970 translation of García Márquez's *Cien años de soledad* (1967)—represents a turning point in the history of translated literature in English, to the extent that the "Boom" also impacted literature originally written in English. According to Lawrence Venuti,

> The English-language success of Latin American writing during the 1960s undoubtedly altered the canon of foreign fiction in British and American cultures, not only by introducing new texts and writers, but by validating experimentalist strategies that undermined the assumptions of classical realism, both theoretical (individualism, empiricism) and ideological (liberal humanism).[1]

Darío, however, who was born in 1868 and died in 1916, lived long before those auspicious years. Prior to 1890, Domingo Faustino Sarmiento's *Facundo* was the only book-length Spanish American work of literary prose translated into English.[2] It was on the year of Darío's death that the first monograph on the region's literature was published, Alfred Coester's pioneering *Literary History of Spanish American Literature*, four years before Isaac Goldberg, another pioneer in the field, published *Studies in Spanish America* (1920).[3] Two years after Darío's death, the first US academic journal devoted to Spanish America, *Hispanic American Historical Review*, was founded in 1918. Sturgis E. Leavitt describes the interest in the region in the early twentieth century as follows:

> As an example of a singular state of ignorance, we note that in 1902 an article in the Literary World of Boston estimates the population of Cuba, Puerto Rico, the Philippines, and Mexico, and says: "It is no exaggeration to say that this mass of our fellow beings have no common literature worthy of that name."[4]

By and large, it was not until the outbreak of the Cuban Revolution in 1959 that readers' attention toward the region resulted in a flurry of translations.

Jeremy Munday proposes that we think of the 1930s as a landmark moment in the history of the translation of Latin American literature.[5] 1930 is the year that Harriet de Onís, the first truly important English-language translator of Latin American novels, published her first translation from the Spanish: *The Eagle and the Serpent* by Martín Luis Guzmán, a novel on the Mexican Revolution. However, according to Deborah Cohn, almost all commercial publishers of the time refused to publish the literature of a region that was practically unknown.[6] Despite Harriet de Onís's outstanding work, it would seem that before the 1960s very few Latin American authors were widely read in Anglo America.[7]

On the other side of the Atlantic, ties with Spanish-language literature in the UK were almost exclusively via Spain until the 1960s. At the University of Oxford, the first official lecturer in Latin American literature was D. P. Gallagher in 1968, whereas the study of Spanish within the framework of the Final Honor School in Modern Languages had begun in 1905. Despite this, Sir Cecil Maurice Bowra, a renowned Oxford classicist and literary critic in the years of post-war Britain, published an essay on Darío in his collection *Inspiration and Poetry* (1955). While at times he commend's Darío's "unfailing technique, excellent ear and abounding vitality," the essay is marred by the author's Eurocentric racism:

> To see him in his right perspective we must remember that he was a stranger from an underdeveloped land, that he had Indian blood in his veins and lacked the complexity and the sophistication which would belong to a European of his gifts and tastes. He differs from European poets of his time because he speaks for human nature at a very simple level and takes things as they come without shaping his life to a plan.[8]

Given Bowra's influence at the time, this undoubtedly did a disservice to Darío's reception in the UK. If we look at other landmarks in the history of Latin American literature in the country, they also seem to point to the Cuban Revolution as a turning point. The Latin American Centre at Oxford was founded in 1964 in St. Anthony's College, though its interest in the region was chiefly historical and political rather than literary, while the Centre for Latin American Studies at Cambridge was established in 1966. Similarly, the Institute of Latin American Studies at London University was founded in 1962.[9] According to Latin Americanists Nikki Craske and David Lehmann,

> By the mid-twentieth century the UK had precious little academic expertise on the region, especially when compared to the Middle East and the former colonies. [...] Latin American literature was scarcely recognized in departments of Spanish—and Rubén Darío was taught as if he was a Spanish poet who just happened to be born in Nicaragua.[10]

If academic interest in the region only gained full-fledged institutional support after 1959, translation however had to exist outside of the academy. While the number of book publications is a reliable measure of the prestige a foreign poet may possess in a literary field (several books by Vallejo have been rendered into English, in addition to an edition of his complete poems), the translation circuit of poetry is different from that of the novel or other genres.[11] Poetry travels more slowly, especially given the rise of the novel as the most popular genre in our literary culture.[12] As predominantly short texts, poems often circulate widely through periodicals and anthologies before they make their way into book-length publications. While the former tend to have a limited and specialized readership, they are nonetheless significant when it comes to understanding a poet's afterlife in English.

The First Translations of Darío

In Leavitt's bibliography of translations and criticism of Spanish American literature published from 1872 to 1932, which includes translations, reviews, articles, history, and textbooks, there are a handful of publications on Darío that appeared during the last years of his life and in the wake of his death, particularly between 1914 and 1919.[13] Perusing those lists of publications, we see that the first endeavors of translating Spanish American poetry into English are bound with the literary projects put forth under the aegis of Pan-Americanism.

As Peter Hulme explains in his work on early twentieth-century Hispanic *Nueva York* and the bilingual poet-translator Salomón de la Selva, the heyday of Pan-Americanism took place between 1898 and 1919. As an ideology, it was the "soothing counter-melody to the strident interventionist tune of US foreign policy."[14] Those were contradictory years for US–Latin America relations. After the Spanish–American War of 1898, Rodó's *arielismo* had taken root among young Spanish American intellectuals: the idea that Latin America was part of a larger family of Latin countries (France, Italy, Spain, among others), whose spiritual conception of life had to be defended against the coarse and rapacious materialism of US imperialism. In an article significantly titled "Literary Yankeephobia in Hispanic America," published in 1922, the early Latin Americanist J. F. Rippy quotes from Goldberg's *Studies in Spanish America* to elaborate on this so-called phobia:

> At best (always speaking generally) we are in their eyes as yet too engrossed in material ambitions to give attention to spiritual considerations; at worst we are the intriguing nation that despoiled Mexico of Texas and California, despoiled Spain of Cuba, despoiled Colombia of Panama, and who now, under the shield of the Monroe Doctrine and an alleged Pan-Americanism, cherish imperialistic designs upon the entire southern continent.[15]

While countries like Nicaragua, the Dominican Republic, and Haiti were under effective US rule by 1915, Pan-Americanism purported to stand for hemispheric brotherhood. In the midst of nationalist and anti-imperialist sentiments articulated through discourses of race, nationality, and culture, earnest Pan-American scholars and translators were in a difficult situation. On the one hand, narratives regarding the superiority of the Anglo-Saxon race, Manifest Destiny, and the Monroe Doctrine buttressed the notion that the US had a right over the countries to its south, enabling a nationalistic disinterest toward foreign literature. Literary critic Albert Mordell put it clearly in a 1922 preface to translator Charles McMichael's book *Reminiscences and Essays* (2022):

> We Americans have often such an overweening pride in our literary superiority that we ignore what our contemporaries in the Latin and South American countries are doing in letters. Dario [sic] visited New York some years ago, and his sojourn there was almost unnoticed.[16]

On the other hand, as a reaction to US interventions, discourses of *arielismo* and pan-Hispanism became extremely popular among Spanish American intellectuals (including Darío), leading to negative prejudices of the United States. Though these views were never unanimous nor straightforward, they shaped the outlook that one side had of the other.[17]

Still, as part of the movement of Pan-Americanism, in addition to numerous conferences being held across the Americas, several periodicals were published with the aim of strengthening the ties among the countries of the hemisphere, several of which were literary. Among these, *Pan-American Poetry, Others*, and specialized issues of *Poetry* and *The Little Review* stand out for the quality of writers from the South, Center, and North of the continent which they brought together.

Others, a small periodical based in New York City, which ran from 1915 to 1919 and some of whose contributors included Ezra Pound, T. S. Eliot, and Marianne More, published a Spanish American number in August 1916, the year of Darío's death, with William Carlos Williams as guest editor.[18] There we find authors such as José Asunción Silva, José Santos Chocano, Leopoldo Lugones, Juan Julián Lastra, Luis Carlos López, and Guillén Zelaya. Despite the timing, there was no sign of Darío. Most of these poets are traditionally classified as *posmodernistas*—late *modernistas* who came after the Nicaraguan poet, with the exception of Asunción Silva. In fact, as we will see, in most of the publications of the time, these late *modernistas* were perceived by US translators and critics as the true representatives of contemporary poetry, whereas Darío belonged to a previous generation of writers.

On the other hand, in the first issue of *Pan-American Poetry* from February 1918, also a small magazine based in New York City, we find Robert Frost, Edna St. Vincent Millay, Amy Lowell, and Carl Sandburg alongside José Santos Chocano, Rubén Darío, Leopoldo Lugones, and Enrique González Martínez.[19] Despite the stellar roster, the magazine lasted only one issue for lack of funds, forcing its editor-in-chief, Salomón de la Selva, to continue his Pan-American translation project merely as a section of the *Pan-American Magazine*, the house journal of the Pan-American Union. In June of that year, de la Selva would publish his rendering in Spanish of a poem by Wallace Stevens, originally titled "Peter Quince at the Clavier." In September, he published another poem by Darío, "Canción de los pinos," rendered into English by Alice Stone Blackwell.[20] Blackwell is Darío's first translator into English, having previously published that same rendering in 1915 in the *New York Evening Post*.[21]

The June 1925 issue of *Poetry* magazine published a selection of verse from most of the countries of Latin America, written by poets such as Gabriela Mistral, Alfonsina Storni, Guillermo Valencia, and others. All were translated by Muna Lee. This included a rendering of Darío, "Litany for Our Lord Don Quixote," in which the Nicaraguan's effortless rhymes appear in stilted English put together in awkward word order. In general, most of the rhyming translations of Darío reveal a pattern whereby the rhymes are achieved at the expense of the other aspects of the poem, especially naturalness of diction, hampering the conveyance of some of Darío's poetic strengths. For instance, the beginning of the poem, "Rey de los hidalgos, señor de los tristes/que de fuerza alientas y de ensueños vistes," is rendered as "King of all cavaliers, lord of the sorrowing/From warfare your sustenance, from dreams your cloak borrowing". (ll. 1–2) The number also featured an introductory note by Harriet Monroe, its editor-in-chief, titled "Pan-American Concord."

Though these early periodical publications, which came about decades before the "Boom," seem to have had no immediate effect on the general perception of Spanish American literature among English-speaking readers of poetry, their historical significance cannot be overstated. As Hulme puts it, "alongside that 1916 Spanish-American issue of *Others*, *Pan-American Poetry* (with its afterlife in the *Pan-American Magazine*) stands as the origin of contemporary translation of poetry from Spanish America into English."[22]

Moreover, recent archival research done by John Alba Cutler shows that hundreds of Darío poems were reprinted in Spanish-language Latino/a serials during the first half of the twentieth century, including several dozen paying homage to his death in 1916, which shows a much larger presence of Darío's work in US magazines and journals at the time than was previously thought.[23] However, the reprintings rediscovered by Alba Cutler were limited to Spanish-language readers in the United States at the time. Like the Pan-American publications, they seemed to have changed little for the general perception of Darío's work.

Hulme puts it bluntly when he claims that, while literary New York was beginning to take Spanish American literature seriously in the first decades of the twentieth century, Darío had simply arrived too early to see it happen. In November 1914, Darío had traveled to the city on an invitation of the Hispanic Society of America, during which he gave a poetry reading and met with local personalities. Hulme quotes essayist Robert Shores's article published shortly after in the Chicago magazine *The Dial*, in which the latter speaks of the ignorance US readers had of foreign literature as "so obvious as to be embarrassing," before adding, "When Señor Rubén Darío arrived in New York not long ago, we went about asking one another, 'Who is this Darío, and what has he done?'"[24] De la Selva relates how they only managed to get an old Chemistry classroom for Darío's poetry reading co-organized by the Hispanic Society of America and Columbia University, during which the poet read for an audience of no more than fourteen.[25]

A trace of his passage through the city can be found in the archive of the *New York Times*: The article "Noted South American Poet Writes about New York" was published on November 29, 1914.[26] The anonymous author describes Darío as the prince of all living poets in the Spanish language, though "little known in this country," comparing his fame to that of Rudyard Kipling in India, before listing the main feats of his diplomatic career and reproducing an abridged and sketch-like English-language version of his essay on Poe from *Los raros*, which contains his first impressions of New York rendered into English. As readers of Darío know, his opinion of the city was not a positive one.

These were also the years in which Spanish American literature, as a subset of Latin American studies, was born as an academic field in the United States. Pedro Henríquez Ureña, who was working at the University of Minnesota at the time, in a letter to Afonso Reyes written on May 12, 1916, describes the state of the art with wry belligerence:

> Aquí no se sabe sino que HAY literatura hispano-americana; pero nadie la ha leído ni piensa leerla, a menos que sepa castellano. En las Universidades la están leyendo, en castellano; existen ya MUCHAS cátedras de literatura hispanoamericana. (...) Pero fuera de las Universidades el público no sabe sino que HAY literatura en la América del Sur.[27]

Despite these circumstances, some book-length translations did come out of these efforts. Albeit more a booklet than a book, Salomón de la Selva and Thomas Walsh's *Eleven Poems* (1916) was published by the Hispanic Society of America the year of Darío's death,[28] the renderings of which I will analyze later. Six years afterward, the translator Charles McMichael published his renderings of Darío titled *Prosas profanas and other poems* (1922)—also more a booklet than a book (nine poems in total). Despite the title, McMichael included a small selection of poems taken not only from *Prosas profanas* but also from *Azul...* and *El canto errante*. Having rendered the poems into prose, they are ripe with mistranslations. A year after its publication, Muna Lee wrote a devastating review in *Poetry* titled "A Painful Example." She describes the booklet as "forced into being with no apparent reason" and calls the preface a burlesque and McMichael a translator unfit for the task.[29]

All in all, considering Pan-American enthusiasm, Darío's celebrity status in the Spanish-speaking world of the time, and the tour he partially carried out in the United States on invitation of the Hispanic Society, the publication of these booklets at the time of his death should be unsurprising. What is surprising, by contrast, is the extent to which they failed to produce any significant interest in his writing, as another book-length translation would not be published until 1965.

Alongside Hulme, scholars such as Soledad Marambio and Harris Feinsod have rescued the work of a whole generation of enthusiastic translators and scholars of poetry who espoused Pan-Americanism and published their renderings before the time of Harriet de Onís:[30] de la Selva, Williams, Muna Lee, Amy Lowell, Luis Muñoz Marín, Alice Blackwell, Isaac Goldberg, and others. Most of them carried out their work in precarious conditions, with little financial support beyond the official institutions of the Pan-American project (The Pan-American Union, the CCLA, the Poetry Society of America, among others). As was perhaps inevitable, Pan-Americanism itself would peter out after 1919 and would eventually disappear with Cold War politics after the Second Great War.

During the roughly forty-year period between 1922 and 1965, Pan-American enthusiasm ended, Good Neighbor diplomacy arose, and poetry anthologies began to emerge in US literary culture. The first anthologists of Spanish American poetry were the Pan-Americanists, who began to publish their collected translations in the 1920s. Thomas Walsh published his own renderings of Darío as part of his mammoth anthology *Hispanic Literature* (1920), which is over 700 pages long and includes a selection of texts that spans from *El Cid* to Muñoz Marín. Not unlike Muna Lee's rendering mentioned previously, the translated poems are full of padding and distortions for the sake of complete rhymes. For example, here is how Walsh renders the first two stanzas of Darío's well-known "Canción de otoño en primavera":[31]

Canción [sic] of Autumn in Springtime

Days of youth, my sacred treasure,
Unreturning ye pass by!—
Would I weep?—no tears I measure;—
Then my tears—I know not why!—

My poor heart hath been divided
In its days celestial here;
There was a gentle maid, unguided
Through this world's afflictions drear; (ll. 1–8).

Compare this with Darío's light and supple Spanish, in which rhymes are effortlessly woven together throughout the poem:

> Juventud, divino tesoro,
> ¡ya te vas para no volver!
> Cuando quiero llorar no lloro
> y a veces lloro sin querer...
>
> Plural ha sido la celeste
> historia de mi corazón.
> Era una dulce niña, en este
> mundo de duelo y aflicción. (ll. 1–8)

The translation falls painfully short of the task of carrying over the poem's richness and musicality.

In 1929, Alice Blackwell put together a lifetime's work of poetry translation and published it as an anthology called *Some Spanish American Poets*, which included 207 poems by eighty-nine authors, among which there are eight poems by Darío. It included a translator's note and a short introduction by Isaac Goldberg, one of the handful of authorities on Spanish American literature in the United States. In her note, Blackwell is all too aware of the scarce knowledge of Spanish American literature at the time, and gives us a notion of the conditions of its reception when she claims that "even to those who are familiar with European literature, the literature of the southern part of our own hemisphere is generally as unknown as the dark side of the moon."[32]

Blackwell is the most successful among these early twentieth-century Darío translators. The poet's concision and naturalness of idiom aren't always carried over, but she manages nevertheless to recreate the rhymes without forcing the other aspects of the poem. The beginning of "Cosas del Cid," for example, from *Prosas profanas*, is translated as follows:[33]

> Stories of the Cid
>
> Barbey narrates, in verse well worth his prose,
> A story of the Cid, fresh as a rose,
> Pure as a pearl. In it we do not hear

Spain's trumpets on the wind ring loud and clear,
Nor do the Moors flee, when day's beams reveal,
Bright in the sun, Tizona's soul of steel. (ll. 1–6)

Blackwell loses the tempo in line four, but otherwise this is a solid rendering of the source poem. The liberties she takes do not lead her to distort the poem's meaning, and she has successfully carried over Darío's playful tone:

Cuenta Barbey, en versos que bien valen su prosa,
una hazaña del Cid, fresca como una rosa,
pura como una perla. No se oyen en la hazaña
resonar en el viento las trompetas de España,
ni el azorado moro las tiendas abandona
al ver al sol el alma de acero de Tizona. (ll. 1–6)

That said, elsewhere she is less successful, such as in "Un soneto a Cervantes" from *Cantos de vida y esperanza*. Here's the octave of Darío's sonnet in Spanish:

Un soneto a Cervantes

Horas de pesadumbre y de tristeza
paso en mi soledad. Pero Cervantes
es buen amigo. Endulza mis instantes
ásperos, y reposa mi cabeza.

Él es la vida y la naturaleza.
Regala un yelmo de oro y diamantes
a mis sueños errantes.
Es para mí. Suspira, ríe y reza. (ll. 1–8)

The simple yet elegant hendecasyllables, with their play of caesura and enjambment, are carried over with padding, expansion, and some rewriting, though the result is not altogether without merit.

Sonnet to Cervantes

Though heavy hours I pass and mournful days
In solitude, Cervantes is to me
A faithful friend. He lightens gloom with glee;
A restful hand upon my head he lays.

> Life in the hues of nature he portrays;
> A golden helmet, jeweled brilliantly,
> He gives my dreams, that wander far and free.
> He suits my moods; he sighs, he laughs, he prays. (ll. 1–8)

Since translating into rhyme was the norm at the time, it was natural that all these translators prioritize it in their versions. Blackwell, however, in her renderings of "Hondas," "A Margarita Debayle," and "La Página Blanca," fails to recreate Darío's experiments with unorthodox rhyme, spacing, and line breaks, giving the English-language reader the image of a more traditional poet than he was. At a time when Modernism was on the rise, this made Darío less attractive for English-language readers.

Furthermore, there is a clue in Goldberg's introduction regarding the reasons behind Darío's obscurity in the decades that followed, especially if we consider the preference for *posmodernistas* mentioned earlier. In his text, Goldberg focuses on the writing of then contemporary poets who came after the Nicaraguan author: González Martínez, Chocano, and Eguren, among others. By the late 1920s, *Modernismo* had changed quickly, and this was reflected in the opinion of these US scholars and translators. Drawing a contrast between Darío's generation and the contemporary one, Goldberg writes:

> It had been the office of early Modernism to assimilate the cosmopolitan currents of the new age; contemporary Modernism—for the era has not really run its course—seeks to direct the continental energies into continental channels.[34]

We find similar undertones in the introduction to another notable anthology of those years: G. Dundas Craig's *The Modernist Trend in Spanish-American Poetry* (1934)—the selection of which begins with José Asunción Silva, includes fourteen translated poems of Darío, and closes with Jorge Luis Borges and Vicente Huidobro. Dundas Craig writes that it "remains true that Darío was a great poet," before adding, "though present tense recoils from the artificiality and preciosity of some of his poems, enough of his work that has permanent value remains for the delight of generations to come."[35] In 1934, Darío was already an object of literary history.

Regarding his translations, Craig explains he has tried to "steer a middle course between the literal prose translation and the poetic paraphrase," ostensibly to reproduce some of the effect of the form of the poem while approximating its meaning.[36] In theory this is all fine and well, except when it's put into practice. As with the previous translators, the search for rhyme overrides everything else, as seen in the following comparison:

> Y tímida ante el mundo, de manera
> Que encerrada en silencio no salía
> Sino cuando en la dulce primavera
> Era la hora de la melodía ... (ll. 25–28)

> So timid 'twas before the world, that never
> It left the silence of its cloister'd pale,
> Unless in dulcet springtime at the hour
> When sweet harmonious music would prevail ... (ll. 25–28)[37]

Craig's unnecessary Latinate words and excessive padding make Darío seem like a lesser poet from a much earlier period.

The volume was praised by Latin Americanists at the time, such as historian Percy Alvin Martin from Stanford University, who warmly welcomed an anthology of this kind in the nascent field of studies. In his enthusiastic review published in *The Hispanic American Historical Review*, he gives us a snapshot of the attitudes toward Spanish American poetry which persisted within academia: "There has long existed among students of Hispanic American history an unfortunate disposition to minimize or ignore the achievements of our southern neighbors in the domain of Belles Lettres."[38] Incidentally, of the anthologies mentioned above, only Blackwell's would be reprinted in 1937 and 1968.

To come back to the generational question, Marambio counts twelve books of Latin American poetry edited in the United States during the next decade (1933–43), of which six are anthologies. Among the remaining six, she finds translated collections of Chocano and Nervo, as well as a book on Carlos Pellicer, Pablo Neruda, and José Carrera Andrade.[39] Clearly, interest lay in *Posmodernismo* and *Vanguardismo*.

These were the years of Good Neighbor Diplomacy. As Feinsod shows, it was a time at which the United States invested heavily in agencies and infrastructure to improve inter-American relations as well as its image abroad: Nelson Rockefeller's Office of the Coordinator of Inter-American Affairs (CIAA) was founded, the Pan-American Highway was completed, as well as Pan American World Airways and a "a Good Neighbor Fleet" of cargo and passenger ships. Inter-American cultural diplomacy developed into a circuity of state agencies and nongovernmental organizations, which included the Committee on Cultural Relations with Latin America (CCRLA), the Council for Pan-American Democracy (CPAD), The Office of War Information (OWI), Voice of America (VOA), and the Pan-American Union (PAU). Good Neighbor diplomacy had a large impact on several types of media (Orson Welles and Walt Disney often come up as examples of film media), including poetry.[40] In fact, Dudley Fitts's landmark anthology *Contemporary Latin American Poetry* from 1942 was commissioned by the CIAA.[41]

At this point, the last book-length publication of Darío's writing had been McMichael's in 1922. Among anthologists and translators, his poetry was perceived as something that made possible, yet came decidedly before, the writings of contemporary Spanish American poets. Fitts takes this as the starting point for his anthology. Modern Spanish American poetry seemed to begin exactly where Darío's ended:

> This anthology is intended as an introductory survey of Latin American poetry since the death, in 1916, of Rubén Darío. The *terminus a quo* was not arrived at arbitrarily. Although the Darío tradition is still very powerful, much of the important poetry written to the south of us during the last quarter century has manifested a strong reaction against it—a reaction prefigured in the sonnet by Enrique González Martínez which serves as epigraph to this volume. The new verse is tougher, more intellectualized; its symbol is the "sapient Owl", as opposed to the graceful but vague and somewhat decadent Swan so beloved by Darío and his precursor among the French symbolists.[42]

Hulme was right—Darío had arrived too early. To illustrate the extent of the anthology's influence, Feinsod mentions how Octavio Paz and José Lezama

Lima continued writing to Fitts long after its publication, thinking that they could enter the US literary marketplace through him.[43]

Another anthology published one year later, *12 Spanish American Poets* (1943), which brought together the renderings of writer and translator H. R. Hays,[44] confirms that Darío had fallen out of the picture. It begins with Mexican poet Ramón López Velarde and includes *vanguardistas* such as the young Borges, Vicente Huidobro, Jorge Carrera Andrade, César Vallejo, and Pablo Neruda. Hays was later credited with having introduced Neruda to US literary circles.[45]

His introductory text to his personal collection of translations shows Hays to be an extraordinary commentator of Spanish American poetry. In quick brush strokes, he touches on the impact of socioeconomic conditions on the development of different genres; key differences between Anglo and Spanish American literatures; the distinct role of poetry and poets within Spanish American culture; the relationship between Spanish American literature and European literature, especially between *Modernismo* and Symbolism; the reception that the latter has had in the hemisphere, which according to Hays is the most striking difference between Anglo and Spanish American poetry at the time; among others.[46] In his account, two movements constitute the background of what was then contemporary Spanish American poetry, which he links to international avant-garde movements such as Surrealism: on the one hand, *Modernismo*, with Darío at its helm; on the other, *Posmodernismo* (or *Mundonovismo*). As in the case of Fitts, at this point Darío and *Modernismo* were relevant only as literary history.

Hays's anthology would have a huge influence on Robert Bly, who claimed Hays had shown him "how wild Neruda was." Thanks to Bly's enthusiasm, the anthology would be republished decades after it had gone out of print, in 1972, with a note on the book jacket that reads: "H.R. Hays is to the translation of South American poetry as Madame Cure is to the x-ray!"[47] Bly would go on to become one of the most prolific and influential translators of the postwar period, rendering poets as diverse as Neruda, Vallejo, Antonio Machado, Georg Trakl, Rainer Maria Rilke, Tomas Tranströmer, and Hafez. Despite his influence and pioneering translation work, as is the case of the Pan-American translators, Hays is scarcely mentioned in histories of translation.

The Surprising Case of Gabriela Mistral

Around the years in which Fitts and Hays published their anthologies, one *posmodernista* became the first Latin American to win a Nobel Prize, and the fifth woman in the prize's history: Chilean poet Gabriela Mistral. It was 1945, the year the Second Great War came to an end; Nazism had been defeated; and yet, the prize went to a South American woman. The Swedish Academy's choice seems to have baffled many in the Global North: though well known across the Spanish-speaking world, Mistral's writing was virtually unknown in the Anglophone world. Writing for *The Nation*, Mildred Adams describes how the news was received in New York: "Her recent elevation to Nobel Prize status was met mostly with a blank stare and interrogative eyebrow."[48]

It's useful to look at Mistral's reception to compare it to Darío's in those years. Unlike the Nicaraguan poet, in the eyes of the translators mentioned above, Mistral was a truly contemporary writer. Her writing was well known in the small circles of Pan-Americanists: after Chocano, she is the best represented poet in Blackwell's *Some Spanish American Poets*, with seventeen of her poems included.

Still, when she was awarded the Nobel prize, there was no book-length publication in English under her name. As Elizabeth Horen explains, Mistral herself was painfully aware of how much weight such things carried when it came to international recognition: were it not for the book-length French translation of her poetry—in the project of which she became heavily involved, choosing the two translators that would render her work—Mistral would have probably never received the Nobel. As she herself commented in a letter in which she points to the politics of translations in international awards: "'La Academia Sueca no puede premiar, ni con su mejor voluntad, a un autor no traducido en libro, al inglés 1º y al francés en segundo términos' (GM/M. Petit, 28 enero 1940)."[49] While Mistral was translated and edited in French with a (albeit ambivalent) preface by Paul Valéry, she would die without seeing her writings in book form rendered into English, the fact of which is telling of the barren publishing landscape for Latin American literature in English translation—with or without a Nobel prize.

After Mistral received the award, Knopf became interested in publishing her work. The translator for the job was to be none other than Harriet de Onís. Though Mistral accepted the offer quickly and enthusiastically, it later transpired that de Onís had backed out of the agreement, claiming to have been burnt out.[50] Marambio mentions that Mistral wanted to select the poems which de Onís was to translate—a task on which the translator, who had only rendered prose at that point, claimed to feel unable to deliver. Still, it's surprising that Knopf did not hire another translator for the publication of a Nobel laureate, which might reflect the little symbolic capital Spanish American letters bore in the English-speaking world. As Marambio explains, with de Onís out of the picture, it would seem that there were no translators available to Knopf at the time (Goldberg had died a few years earlier, Blackwell was nearly blind). Poetry was on the decline, whereas the novel, which was preferred by Knopf as part of their editorial line, was selling increasingly well. By contrast, Latin American literature was selling poorly, a situation which remained unchanged throughout the years leading to the "Boom."

When other publishing houses got wind that the agreement with Knopf had fallen through, both Farrar, Straus and Co. and Random House showed interest. Nonetheless, these agreements would also be frustrated given issues with the translations. In the former case, Katherine Biddle, the translator hired by Farrar, Straus and Co. to do the translations, suddenly left the country and seems to have gradually abandoned the project. In the latter case, Mistral was unhappy with Eleanor Turnbull's renderings, who had been hired for the job and whose versions did not convince the editors at Random House either. The need for a poet with some knowledge of Spanish is mentioned in the correspondence between them, but the Nobel laureate would die before any other translator was found.[51]

Shortly after her death, the poet Langston Hughes would publish his renderings of her poetry. In the introduction to his translations, he comments on the following:

> Although her first publication was achieved in our country, in Continental Europe her poems were more widely translated than in England or the United States. Even after she was awarded the Nobel Prize for Literature, why so little of Gabriela was translated into English, I do not know.[52]

The first publication that Hughes mentions was thanks to Blackwell's dutiful renderings, undoubtedly a pioneer in the translation of Spanish American literature into English.

The case of Mistral illustrates and confirms both the limitations of periodical publications for the widespread recognition of a poet's work, as well as the little interest in Spanish American literature that existed before the "Boom," despite the effort of some maverick translators and poets. The fact that she died a Nobel laureate without having a book under her name in English underlines the starkness of the situation.

Looking at this period from a different angle, the interim between 1922 and 1965 can also be seen as roughly overlapping with the rise and ensuing canonization of Anglo-American and British Modernism for English-language literature. If we compare the poetics of Ezra Pound, T. S. Eliot, or William Carlos Williams with the English-speaking Darío we have so far analyzed, the differences are vast. As mentioned earlier, Modernism not only changed literature originally written in English, but it also brought about significant changes for the genre of translated poetry.

According to Venuti, the experimentation that came about with Modernism brought with it innovative forms of translation that challenged what he calls "the dominance of transparent discourse in English-language translation." In other words, it questioned the predominance of certain conventions in translated literature whose origin he traces back to the Early Modern period, according to which translations were valued on the basis of their fluency and assimilation to local poetics (what is otherwise known as "domestication").[53] As André Lefevere points out, these conventions have often led to baffling contradictions, such as the insistence on the part of reviewers that classical authors like Homer and Horace should be translated into rhyme to be rendered more faithfully, even if neither the Ancient Greeks nor the Romans wrote in rhyme. In the words of Lefevere,

> Many nineteenth-century translations of Catullus [...] rhyme, even though the original does not. The need to rhyme, therefore, by no means comes out of the "structure" of the original; quite the contrary. It is imposed on translators by the "translation poetics" of their day, which in the nineteenth century held that acceptable poetry translations should make use of the

illocutionary strategies of meter and rhyme. Translation poetics, like all poetics, tend to change over the years.[54]

When Modernism came about, it questioned the dominance of that convention. However, by the early 1950s, free verse and precise current language were established as the conventional poetic idiom. Also, the translated text of poetry had gained aesthetic autonomy: it could now be read on its own.[55] These new conventions came to be established through the success of works such as Pound's *Cathay*, published in 1915.

In addition to the perception of Darío as a figure of mostly historical interest which we see in translation anthologies of the period, if we take this poetic shift as the backdrop against which renderings such as de la Selva and Walsh's were read, they must have come across as something belonging to the Anglo-American and British nineteenth century. This situation is further compounded by the distinct historical developments that both literary traditions, in English and in Spanish, underwent at the turn of the century.

Modernism and Modernismo

Caught between the throes of a declining empire and the paucity of the incipient postcolonial nations of the Americas, Spanish-language literature had stagnated in the nineteenth century. Faced with this reality, *modernistas* strove to enter the wider conversation of the West by fast-forwarding the development of their literature. As a result, in *modernista* poetry, several literary schools appear collapsed into one: it drew not only from Romanticism (early Darío is a Romantic poet) but from *Parnasse, Décadentisme, Symbolisme*, and British Pre-Raphaelitism, in addition to the writings of Edgar Allan Poe and Walt Whitman. However, these precipitous changes took place at the end of the nineteenth century, before Pound and Eliot arrived in England in the early twentieth century. In fact, as Hays asserts in his introduction to his translations, Modernism entered the conversation of *fin-de-siècle* literature— which was already taking place in France, in Latin America, in Spain, in Portugal, in Italy, and in Germany—rather late.[56] Peter Childs's account of English literature at the time is worth quoting in full:

At the time of this steady increase in outside influence on literature up to the Great War, English poetry was at one of its lowest points, according to many critics. Prior to the changes in diction and subject matter achieved by the well-known war poets, such as Isaac Rosenberg, Wilfred Owen and Edward Thomas, many of whom were not highly regarded until the 1930s, poetry was deeply conservative and insular. A large number of the prominent names of the Edwardian period are now nearly forgotten: William Watson, W.E. Henley, Laurence Binyon and Alfred Austin (Poet Laureate from 1896 to 1913). Unless it is by the Romantic-turned-modernist W.B. Yeats, the poetry of the pre-war period most likely to be studied now was written by two independent-minded and highly individualistic poets better known to the public for their fiction: Thomas Hardy (1840–1928), whose influence on modern British poetry has been as great as anyone's, and Rudyard Kipling (1865–1936), probably the most popular literary writer of the period.[57]

Nevertheless, when Modernism did enter the conversation, it did so sweepingly, with novel poetic principles and groundbreaking experimentation that would change the face of English-language literature and beyond.

Chronologically, Modernism took root when the *Vanguardias* were doing so in Spanish America—its proverbial *annus mirabilis*, 1922, is also the year Vallejo's *Trilce* was published, as well as Oliverio Girondo's *Veinte poemas para ser leídos en el tranvía*, Salomón de la Selva's *Un soldado desconocido,* and Manuel Maples Arce's *Andamios interiores (poemas radiográficos)*. It was also the year when the magazine *Proa* was founded in Buenos Aires by Jorge Luis Borges, and *Actual. Hoja de vanguardia* by the *estridentistas* in Mexico City. Still, *Modernismo* and Modernism shared influences, such as *Décadentisme* and *Symbolisme*, and both looked to Paris as their artistic capital, not to mention their common aim to be modern and renew their respective literary traditions.[58] For this reason, a long-standing debate exists as to whether *Modernismo* can be understood as a kind of Hispanic Modernism.

Among recent Darío translators, Derusha and Acereda refer to *Modernismo* as Hispanic Modernism, ostensibly on the basis that as literary movements both represent each tradition's response to modernity. Other writers and critics, such as Octavio Paz, reject the equation and propose instead that the Latin American equivalent of Modernism is the *Vanguardias*, whereas *Modernismo* would be an equivalent of *Parnasse* and *Symbolisme*.[59] This seems overly chronological. A third position in the debate comprises an altogether different critical strand that dates to Spanish writer Juan Ramón Jiménez, and was later developed by critics such as Federico de Onís, Iván Schulman, and Ricardo Gullón. These critics view *Modernismo* as an irrevocable change of paradigm that is almost commensurate with modernity itself, whose multiple manifestations (*Modernismo*, Modernism, *Modernité*, etc.) share the same root. According to these scholars, we still have not lived through the end of *Modernismo*. While this latter view has the advantage of hinting at the global dimension of modernization in its form of industrial and postindustrial capitalism, it fails to account for the differences between traditions and indeed between literary movements within the same language. As Alejandro Mejías-López argues, the narrative is also underpinned by Spanish colonial anxieties at the turn of the century, as it conveniently presents *Modernismo* as a simultaneous pan-Hispanic opening-up to other European literatures, and not as a movement which was originally Spanish American.[60]

Arthur Symons's influential *The Symbolist Movement in Literature* of 1899, later expanded with added essays and translations in 1908 and 1919, is perhaps the most important English-language document to attest to the commonalities between movements. As is well known, it would become formative reading for some of the most important modernist writers, namely William Butler Yeats, T. S. Eliot, and James Joyce.[61] Symons's book is worth analyzing in detail because it gives us a glimpse of how the French *fin de siècle*, as a body of literary works, was read differently by modernists and *modernistas*. It is a key text to understand how their readings diverge significantly despite their common subject matter. In between Symons's lines we can make out omissions and emphases that would be decisive for the development of modern poetry in English. As Creasy explains, "*The Symbolist Movement* [...] does not simply mediate between French literature and English speakers; it mediates between the *fin de siècle* and Modernism."[62] It does so because it is idiosyncratic as literary history, something which Eliot later commented on in his own critical writings.[63] It fashions its own image of French literature, leaving out some writers relevant for *Symbolisme* and disdaining others.

Jean Moréas is a case in point. As the author of the symbolist manifesto, Moréas was greatly influential for Darío and *Modernismo* at large, both for his early writings as well as his later classicism. By contrast, Symons only mentions him once in his work, and does so through the following caricature:

> In this hazardous experiment [the book *Le Pèlerin passionné*] M. Jean Moréas, whose real talent lies in quite another direction, has brought nothing into literature but an example of deliberate singularity for singularity's sake. I seem to find the measure of the man in a remark I once heard him make in a café, where we were discussing the technique of metre: "You, Verlaine!" he cried, leaning across the table, "have only written lines of sixteen syllables; I have written lines of twenty syllables!"
>
> That is indeed the measure of the man, and it points a criticism upon not a few of the busy little *littérateurs* who are founding new *revues* every other week in Paris. These people have nothing to say, but they are resolved to say something, and to say it in the newest mode. They are Impressionists because it is the fashion, Symbolists because it is the vogue, Decadents because Decadence is in the very air of the cafés. And so, in their manner, they are mile-posts on the way of this new movement, telling how far it has gone.[64]

Elsewhere, Symons brushes *Décadentisme* aside, presenting it as nothing else than a forerunner to Symbolism:

> Meanwhile, something which is vaguely called Decadence had come into being. That name, rarely used with any precise meaning, was usually either hurled as a reproach or hurled back as a defiance. [...] But a movement which in this sense might be called Decadent could but have been a straying aside from the main road of literature. [...] The interlude, half a mock-interlude, of Decadence, diverted the attention of the critics while something more serious was in preparation.[65]

Scholars have in recent years reevaluated the importance of *Décadentisme*.[66] Murray Pittock points out that Symons's downgrade of *Décadence* as a passing phase in Symbolism's development is often wrongly assumed to be a judicious observation, ignoring that Symons's text originally discussed *Décadence* in the same terms in which he later did *Symbolisme*. However, Symons changed the term because of the moral implications that the word "Decadence" had acquired in the latter half of the 1890s in the aftermath of Oscar Wilde's infamous trial.⁶⁷ In Pittock's account, Symon's far-reaching influence includes not only the very definition of Symbolism in literature, but also his rescue of the Metaphysical Poets and his idea of Donne as in a "morbid state of body and brain and nerves," despite all his contradictions, prejudices and "opportunistic changes of heart of which Symons's arguments were guilty."⁶⁸ As Creasy points out, Symons's understanding of French *Symbolisme* was mostly retrospective.⁶⁹ Of the writers he discussed, only Maeterlinck and Huysmans were alive when he first published his book.⁷⁰ By contrast, when Darío published *Los raros*, half of the authors he eulogized were still living. Inevitably, both authors lagged behind Paris. Nonetheless, Darío had followed the vicissitudes of French literature since at least the mid-1880s, when *Azul …* (1888) was published in Chile. It is for this reason that his own image of French poetry included *Parnasse*, which, in Symons's view, was already something of the past.

Symons puts forth a narrative in which *Décadence*, which largely overlapped with *Symbolisme* in the *fin de siècle*, was superseded by the latter. In time, as Sherry points out, "the inventiveness of modernism [would be attached] to the theory of novelty in symbolism and detach[ed] from the mood of decadence."⁷¹ As a result, a great deal of the vocabulary of forms and tropes which *Parnasse* represented for Darío would have become, in the eyes of the modernists who read Symons, antiquated. In other words, in a matter of a few decades, Darío's modernity stopped being modern. To name but one example, the craftsmanship that Parnassians raised against their predecessors the Romantics posited the structure of poetry as inextricable from rhyme.

While Darío indeed embodies the most far-reaching period of renovation in Spanish-language verse, he seldom wrote in free verse. His wide-ranging innovations, rather than *vers libre*, can be classified as *vers libéré* or *vers libres classiques*.⁷² That is, as a liberated form of regular verse that plays with caesura, enjambment, line length, and rhyming structure, but which maintains the indispensability of rhyme and, more often than not, isosyllabism.⁷³ With the establishment of free verse as the main poetic idiom, this position quickly became outdated, even unmodern. Coupled with his Parnassian mythological tropes, this would make Darío seem *passé* when read through a modernist lens.⁷⁴ Likewise, the painters to whom he felt closest were part of the nineteenth-century *art nouveau* movement, not impressionists or expressionists. As Nicaraguan poet Carlos Martínez Rivas explains:

> *Sus* pintores —no precisamente porque los mencione con mayor o menor frecuencia, sino porque saturan e impregnan su prosa y poesía— son, en mi opinión, tres: Watteau, Moreau y el movimiento art nouveau, representado y dominado original y magistralmente, entre 1894 y 1898, por Aubrey Beardsley.[75]

Darío's reaction to Auguste Rodin's sculpture is illustrative of his aesthetics, which can be found in two essays from *Peregrinaciones* (1901). His teetering ambivalence comes through in several passages. He is torn when it comes to taking a position before the scandals roused by Rodin's sculptures:

> Yo expondré, con toda la transparencia de que me siento capaz, este resumen: he hallado a dos Rodines: un Rodin maravilloso de fuerza y de gracia artística, que domina a la inmediata, vencedor en la luz, maestro plástico y prometeico encendedor de vida, y otro Rodin cultivador de la fealdad, torturador del movimiento, incomprensible, excesivo, ultraviolento, u obrando a veces *como entregado a esa cosa extraña que se llama la casualidad*.[76]

It is the latter Rodin, the sculptor of tortuous and lopsided statuary, who made Darío uncomfortable. Harmony and symmetry, aesthetic values that were also at the heart of Parnassian craftsmanship, gave way to the representation of the swirling violence of life in the French sculptor's later work. Groping for a model against which to measure the Frenchman's artistic value, Darío cannot help but compare him with the masters of Ancient Greece:

> Pero, ante todo, debo declarar que no concibo en Rodin un representativo del espíritu griego; Rodin no tiene de Grecia más que el concepto de la tragedia; es la máscara trágica la que le obsede. [...] Pero no hay en él la virtud olímpica de Fidias, de Praxíteles, de los antiguos maestros helenos.[77]

For all of what is often called its revolutionary effects, the aesthetics of *Modernismo* had a classicist root, as was inevitable when influenced by *Parnasse*.[78] As discussed in Chapter 2, once *Symbolisme* had come to an end, classical sources would figure more prominently in the poetry of Darío. Still, while he could not bring himself to enjoy Rodin's later work, he sensed that it was likely to break a path. The following passage discussing the Frenchman's sculpture of Balzac exemplifies his earnest effort to understand the furor caused by the piece:

> No, decididamente, después de tomar por varios caminos, no entiendo del todo. Se trata de la más plástica de las artes. ¿Para qué haber modelado de antemano con loable tenacidad [la] anatomía del autor de la Comedia Humana para venir a presentar esa cara deforme y esos grandes pies que se escapan de esa salida de baño? Miro de frente, y un profundo respeto por el genial artista no contiene la vaga sonrisa que se escurre a la violenta imposición de un aspecto de foca. ¡Deliberadas faltas de ortografía del Arte! *M'introdui en ton histoire* … [sic] Miro detrás y la masa inclinada clama por un puntal. Miro de lado y el dolmen elefantino se obstina en no querer revelarme su secreto. Entonces, con resolución completa, no me acepto a mí mismo, me increpo y me llamo en alemán bildungphilister [sic], para castigarme por el lado de Nietzsche. Persisto en creer en la lealtad de Rodin. Sacerdote de la síntesis, nos habrá querido dar la esfinge moderna o la fórmula de un arte futuro.[79]

The passage is revealing also in its ironic self-admonishment for not being able to understand the work, to the extent of calling himself in Nietzschean terms *ein Bildungsphilister*—a narrow-minded snob. It shows Darío's intuition of the value of Rodin's legacy.[80]

Such intimations, which arose amid the frustration at not understanding some of the latest tendencies in European art, also appear in Darío's appraisal of Filippo Tommaso Marinetti and Arthur Rimbaud. As he did with Rodin, Darío goes back to the classics when he reviews Marinetti's futurist manifesto, debunking the Italian's claim to novelty by quoting the text and ironically glossing upon it:

> 1. «Queremos cantar el amor del peligro, el hábito de la energía y de la temeridad.»
>
> En la primera proposición paréceme que el futurismo se convierte en pasadismo. ¿No está todo eso en Homero?

2. «Los elementos esenciales de nuestra poesía serán el valor, la audacia y la rebeldía.» ¿No está todo eso ya en todo el ciclo clásico?

3. «Habiendo hasta ahora magnificado la literatura la inmovilidad pensativa, el éxtasis y el sueño, queremos exaltar el movimiento agresivo, el insomnio febriciente [sic], el paso gimnástico, el salto peligroso, la bofetada y el puñetazo.» Creo que muchas cosas de esas están ya en el mismo Homero, y que Píndaro es un excelente poeta de los deportes.[81]

At the same time, he applauds Marinetti's enthusiasm and admires the thrust of his style:

En su violencia, aplaudo la intención de Marinetti, porque la veo por su lado de obra de poeta, de ansioso y valiente poeta que desea conducir el sagrado caballo hacia nuevos horizontes. Encontraréis en todas esas cosas mucho de excesivo; el son de guerra es demasiado impetuoso; pero ¿quiénes sino los jóvenes, los que tienen la primera fuerza y la constante esperanza, pueden manifestar los intentos impetuosos y excesivos?[82]

Though he ultimately rejected the tenets of futurism, he still recognized its aesthetic potential.

Likewise, when in 1913 Darío reviewed an Italian biography on Rimbaud written by Ardengo Soffici, he showed bewilderment redolent of his reaction before Rodin's *Balzac*, along with a similar intuition of its aesthetic importance:[83]

El talento de Rimbaud se desarrolló, escribe muchas de sus mejores poesías y las *Iluminaciones,* poema en prosa, de una inaudita concepción y de más que inaudita factura. Yo confieso que hay cosas que no comprendo en absoluto sino en sentido de sugestión musical. En veces se cree, vislumbrar el genio —y cosa bien natural—, no se asombra uno mucho, por lo tanto, en otras ocasiones, de pensar en la locura ...[84]

On the one hand, the fact that Darío can only follow Rimbaud "en sentido de sugestión musical" reveals the limits of his conception of poetry, greatly influenced by *Parnasse* as mentioned earlier, in which musicality is the most important feature. On the other hand, the suggestion of madness in an artist whose work seemed unintelligible was commonplace in the *fin de siècle*. It's a standard reaction for the time. He then adds: "Imposible analizar en estas harto limitadas líneas la extraordinaria, desbocada, hermética, relampagueante, desconcertante creación rimbaudina."[85] Clearly, he is nevertheless enthused by Rimbaud.

One of the things that puzzled Darío of the French poet's life was his renouncement of his privileged position within French literature, a reaction which bespeaks the cultural anxieties inherent to the postcolonial predicament of Spanish American writers at the time:

> Ahora bien, lo prodigioso, lo portentoso de ese niño enfermo, es que en lo mejor de su juventud arrojó su talento, su genio, al olvido. Y se fue. Se fue de Francia para países extraños. Sin un céntimo. A ser comerciante, traficante, qué sé yo, en pueblos africanos, a sufrir temperaturas imposibles y a realizar esta cosa que resiste a todas las fuerzas de su voluntad: olvidar a París.[86]

What Darío cannot bring himself to understand is how someone could reject the cultural capital that Paris offers, for which he longed all his life. Still, it was Verlaine who remained Darío's poetic hero, not Rimbaud. In Symons's eyes, it was also Verlaine who represented the culmination of poetry, not Rimbaud, as was the case for most of those who followed French poetry before Modernism rewrote the canon of *Symbolisme*.[87] And yet, as is well known, it is Rimbaud who has proved more influential for modern poetry. His prose poetry and his experiments in *vers libre* would go on to influence not only surrealists worldwide, but major late twentieth-century poets such as John Ashbery.

While Darío's position regarding the emerging European avant-gardes was reactionary, it would be simplistic to conclude, as Bowra did, that Darío was not sophisticated enough to understand the innovative work of his European counterparts. In an article in which she analyzes Darío's reactions to Rodin, Beatriz Colombi argues that though they share certain motifs (the theme of erotic love and sex, male and female fauns, tritons, Venus, Adonis, Apollo, etc.), it's their notion of form that sets them apart and which reveals "esa modernidad desfasada y de tiempos discontinuos de la que ambos participan."[88] The *desfasamiento* of modernity, or time-lag, a notion which Colombi draws from Homi K. Bhabha's *The Location of Culture* (1994), implies the existence of different and discontinuous historical timelines between literatures.[89] It certainly is a lag of some sort, and not merely the coexistence of independent traditions, because Darío, Marinetti, Rodin, and Rimbaud were all part of a cultural field whose navel, in the nineteenth century, was Paris—a field which since then has increasingly found itself caught in the wheels of post-industrial capitalism, tending toward homogenization and centralization, so that what is modern and new in the literary powerhouses of the West is more desirable than what is local or traditional elsewhere. In this regard I am sympathetic to Frederic Jameson's thinking on the topic, for whom there is a "single" modernity (global capitalism) which manifests itself unevenly and in irreducibly distinct ways across the globe.[90] This explains why literary cultures that share a similar ideology and cohabitate one space may develop and hold different cultural and aesthetic values at the same point in time, as the cases of Rodin and Darío exemplify. And yet a kind of teleology of modernity always comes into play, thanks to which some writers who were once considered modern may cease to be so in a short span of time, superseded by new, inevitably more modern writers.

In the Spanish language, after its relatively modest Romanticism and the prolonged stagnation of its literary resources, there was much to do by way of *vers libéré*, especially regarding metrical exploration and prosodic experiments. *Vers libre* was not a priority at that point in time. In this sense, the failure to understand the circumstances particular to each literature, to read each literary culture on its own terms and according to its own history, and not in relation to another hegemonic tradition, is a common mistake that has led many Spanish American writers to understand the *modernistas* poorly. The debate between Spanish poet Luis Cernuda and Nicaraguan poet-scholar Ernesto Mejía Sánchez exemplifies the situation. In that exchange, Mejía Sánchez replies to Cernuda's contemptuous judgments about Darío, exposing the lacunae in the Spaniard's knowledge of *Modernismo*, as well as shedding light on the historical context in which Darío wrote. For its synthesis and accuracy, his reply is worth quoting in full:

> Entre las influencias, de mayor a menor, suelen citarse Mendés, Banville, Gautier, circunscritas a breves períodos, y otras a meras contaminaciones esporádicas: Moreas [sic], Du Plessis, días de la école romaine. A Baudelaire

no le debe más que ciertos contactos satánicos, pero lo cita de memoria. A Mallarmé lo conoció bien, lo tradujo, hizo un pastiche muy intencionado a su muerte. Y nada más. A Rimbaud lo cita poco, como se lo citaba entonces en Francia. A qué tanto reclamo. Francia era "la Francia" en ese momento y todos los caminos conducían a ella. A través de ella se conoce a Heine, a Poe, a Whitman, a Ibsen, a Tolstoi, a D'Annunzio y a Marinetti.[91]

The *modernistas* knew full well of the existence and possibilities of *vers libre*. Still, they preferred rhyme. Discussing Jean Moréas in *Los raros*, Darío broaches the subject:

> Es innegable que la orquestación exquisita del verso libre, "la máquina del poema poliformo modernísimo", son esfuerzos que seducen; mas es irresistible aquella magia, de los vuelos de palomas, de las frescas rosas, bien rimadas en estrofas harmónicas —la consonancia dulce de los labios, luciente de los ojos, ideal y celeste de las alas y el lenguaje de la pasión y de la juventud.[92]

These poetic divergences become a problem of reception when it comes to reading Darío in English during the early twentieth century. Aside from the fact that there was no readership for Spanish American literature at the time, and that the translations published were of arguable success, it might well be that de la Selva and Walsh's Darío became outdated shortly after its publication. Both translators at the time were poets who were writing verse that was decidedly not modernist. On the one hand, Thomas Walsh was a US poet who wrote Browningesque poems, the themes of which ranged from Catholic faith to the history of Spain. On the other hand, Salomón de la Selva, only twenty-three at the time, was a Nicaraguan-born poet who had moved to the United States some nine years earlier. *Eleven Poems* is actually de la Selva's first published book, in which his uncertain command of English-language verse is apparent.

As the work of a Nicaraguan living in the United States and writing in English, de la Selva's oeuvre can be viewed as embodying the discontinuity between Spanish- and English-language traditions. His first collection of poetry, *Tropical Town and Other Poems* (1918)—which was written in English and published two years after his translations of Darío—is stylistically close to *Posmodernismo*. Pedro Henríquez Ureña describes de la Selva as essentially a poet of the nineteenth century, whose aspirations begin in Keats and Shelley and go as far as Francis Thompson and Alice Meynell.[93] One might also add that de la Selva's first book was staunchly anti-modernist.[94] The collection was written at a time when the Nicaraguan was greatly influenced by Darío and Edna St. Vincent Millay, the latter of whom defended poetic traditionalism against the experimentalism of the modernists. De la Selva counted himself among the writers who advocated a return to the traditional forms of English poetry and opposed what he saw as an ephemeral trend in US poetry.[95]

In contrast, his second collection of poetry was written in Spanish and published four years later as *El soldado desconocido* (1922), which is considered one of the masterpieces of Central American poetry. Unlike his first poetry collection, this Spanish-language collection is indeed modernist; it's perhaps the first Spanish-language work written in that manner. In an article titled "Nota sobre la otra vanguardia," the Mexican writer José Emilio Pacheco posits that there is a second *vanguardia* in the history of Spanish American literature, not so much influenced by European avant-gardes, but by Modernism, or what Pacheco calls North American "New Poetry." He traces this movement back to de la Selva's *El soldado desconocido*, alongside two other works:

> Junto a la vanguardia que encuentra su punto de partida en la pluralidad de «ismos» europeos, aparece en la poesía hispanoamericana otra corriente: casi medio siglo después será reconocida como vanguardia y llamada «antipoesía» y «poesía conversacional», dos cosas afines, aunque no idénticas. Esta corriente, realista y no surrealista, se origina en la «New Poetry» norteamericana. Aparece de manera tan subrepticia que ni siquiera sus introductores se dan cuenta de lo que han aportado. [...] Sus fundadores son un dominicano, Pedro Henríquez Ureña (1884–1946); un nicaragüense, Salomón de la Selva (1893–1959), y un mexicano, Salvador Novo (1904–1974). Sus libros claves se llaman *El soldado desconocido, Espejo, Poemas proletarios* y la primera Antología de la poesía norteamericana moderna, que aparece en español. [...] Así, *El soldado desconocido*, al incorporar el prosaísmo de la new poetry, introduce también las antigüedades modernizadas por Ezra Pound y otros poetas del renacimiento norteamericano.[96]

Pacheco's thesis has prompted critics to begin to reevaluate the significance of de la Selva's oeuvre; by and large, however, this revaluation remains to be completed. I propose that we think of the changes de la Selva's poetry underwent as successively embodying the discontinuities of the two *modernidades* between which he found himself: in other words, it was *modernista* before it became modernist. Ironically, in doing so he inverted the relation between language and aesthetics: he was a *modernista* in English and a modernist *en español*.

This troubled relationship to Modernism makes him an unlikely candidate to have ushered Darío into English successfully. Be that as it may, the role aesthetic and poetic differences play in the reception of translations may not be as large as that of historical and cultural factors. This is especially evident in the translations carried out by the Deep Image poets.

Deep Image Poet-translators and the Rise of the Latin American Poetry Anthology

During the 1950s and the decades that followed, authors such as Robert Bly, James Wright, Clayton Eshleman, Robert Kelly, Jerome Rothenberg, and others sought to reinvigorate US poetry by incorporating elements of the "revolutionary" writing of foreign poets such as Pablo Neruda and César Vallejo. They did so to counter the influence of Poundian imagism, which according to these writers lacked psychological depth. What came about is traditionally known as the Deep Image movement in poetry.

Upon studying the history of the translations of Neruda, Johnathan Coen sees the mid-fifties as a turning point: the practice of rendering Neruda changed from metaphrase to deliberate efforts to revitalize US poetry through the rendering of the Chilean author.[97] Just as for Pound before them, for poet-translators such as Bly, Eshleman, and Ben Belitt, translation became an apprenticeship in the craft of verse and a means by which to learn new registers and images for one's own poetry. Their renderings, however, were often marked by "a disregard for the idioms, cultural associations, intertextuality, and cultural-situatedness of Spanish-language verse."⁹⁸ Belitt, for example, translates Neruda's opening two stanzas of "Walking around" as follows:

> It so happens I'm tired of just being a man.
> I go to a movie, drop in at the tailor's—it so happens—
> feeling wizened and numbed, like a big, wooly swan,
> awash on an ocean of clinkers and causes.
>
> A whiff from the barbershop does it: I yell bloody murder.
> All I ask is a little vacation from things: from boulders and woolens,
> from gardens, institutional projects, merchandise,
> eyeglasses, elevators—I'd rather not look at them. (ll. 1–8)

When compared to the source text, we see how Belitt has almost riffed on Neruda's lines to write a poem with a distinct poetic voice and its own tone, mood, and imagery:

> Sucede que me canso de ser hombre.
> Sucede que entro en las sastrerías y en los cines
> marchito, impenetrable, como un cisne de fieltro
> navegando en un agua de origen y ceniza.
>
> El olor de las peluquerías me hace llorar a gritos.
> Sólo quiero un descanso de piedras o de lana,
> sólo quiero no ver establecimientos ni jardines,
> ni mercaderías, ni anteojos, ni ascensores. (ll. 1–8)

His creativity is commendable, but the divergence from Neruda's source text is significant.

One can also find several mistranslations in the work of these translators given how poor their Spanish was: Bly translates line 3 from the poem above as "dried up, waterproof, like a swan made of felt," the literalism of which is disconcerting; in their rendering of "Melancolía en las familias" by Neruda, "tienda" is translated by Bly and Wright as "grocery store," when it should clearly be "tent"; Merwin renders "la noche está estrellada," from the second line of Neruda's famous "Poema XX," as "the night is shattered"; and Eshelman infamously added expletives to a Vallejo poem where it did not have them, in line with the masculinist poetics that these poets pursued.[99] In the writings of these US authors, Neruda was exoticized as "wild," "masculine," and "earthy," whereas Bly writes of Vallejo's "wildness and savagery."[100]

The widespread neglect of key features of the Spanish-language texts raises questions about the way translation may be carried out when the translators work from within hegemonic literary cultures with a self-serving creative aim. However, as Rachel Galvin explains, the different magazines edited by the Deep Image poets, first *The Fifties* and then *The Sixties*, successfully created a readership for Neruda, Vallejo, and other Spanish-language poets which were published as part of their issues. In stark contrast to the case of Darío or Mistral, by the mid-sixties Neruda was one of the most popular poets in the United States.[101] Galvin judiciously sums up the boons and banes of the situation:

> The translations of Bly, Wright, and Eshelman may be appropriative, prone to deforming tendencies, and conditioned by cultural bias and geopolitical privilege, but we must understand the Deep Image poetic as resulting from its relation to the work of Neruda and Vallejo, regardless of how idiosyncratically it is translated.[102]

Galvin's reckoning reminds us how, despite their erring, these renderings register a relation or a point of contact with Spanish American poetry. One could go further and underline the strictly creative role that translation plays within a literary culture, beyond the ethics and politics it inheres as cultural practice.

For these poets, a translated poem had to work as a poem on its own, which means adapting it to the idioms and conventions in which they were fluent. Therefore, distortions and divergences were inevitable. When they produced their versions, they were not thinking of Spanish but rather English-language readers.

Despite their relationality to the Spanish-language source texts, in the end Merwin's Neruda and Bly's Vallejo are part of US poetry, not Spanish American, which leads us to the question of what these translators were striving to achieve with their renderings. In any case, these translations created a readership for these Spanish American poets and put new voices, images, metaphors, and texts in circulation among US poetry readers.

During the post-war period, along with Deep Image Poet's engagement with the craft of translation, the specifically Latin American poetry anthology became so influential that US poet Kenneth Koch parodied it in a series of pseudo-translations called "Some South American Poets." Indeed, after canonization parody ensues. Published as part of the collection *The Pleasures of Peace* (1969), Koch's parodic exercise includes the poems of fictional, generic, haphazard South American poets vaguely reminiscent of Borges, whose verse is heavy with non-sequiturs and "translatese," such as in the poem "Calle Rosa." It appears as part of the fictional collection *The Streets of Buenos Aires* by fictional poet Jorge Guinhieme:[103]

> Roseway, oh lovely girl,
> Your face is like a tulip.
> I have tulip too, my lovely girl,
> And happily will mingle them with yours. (ll. 1–4)

Scott Douglas Challener has studied the Latin American literature anthology as a genre that transformed US poetry during the post-war period. In addition to Koch's parody, he mentions Jack Spicer's first book of poetry, *After Lorca* (1972), as an example of publications that bear the direct influence of Spanish-language translation anthologies—in the latter case, specifically Donald Allen and Federico García Lorca's co-edited *Selected Poems of Federico García Lorca* (New Directions Press, 1955).

As in the case of Neruda and Vallejo, Lorca was thoroughly Americanized in translation. As Johnathan Mayhew explains in his study *Apocryphal Lorca: Translation, Parody, Kitsch* (2009), during the 1950s and 1960s, the Spanish poet was rendered a specifically US figure who was "adaptable to the cultural and ideological desiderata of the U.S. poets during the cold war period."[104]

Though these publications indicate radically different circumstances for the reception of Spanish American poetry in the United States in the second half of the twentieth century, the role anthologies play in a literary field is complex.[105] On the one hand, all translation distorts the context of a text—and translation anthologies do so even more. As Douglas Challener explains, these do not simply reproduce poems, but "address them to new publics, and in doing so, project new discursive contexts for the socioformal relations that cut across and against individual poems."[106] On the other hand, anthologies in themselves are canon-defining texts, which decisively shape the narrative of literary history through an interplay of inclusions and exclusions.

In the case of Darío, from Fitt's anthology on, whenever he was included, he was presented as a poet whose value is first and foremost historical: on the one hand, he was put forth as the most influential of Spanish American poets and the initiator of its modernist renewal; yet, on the other, as one whose poetry was decidedly not contemporary. Also, the versions through which he was rendered failed to convey the most important features of his poetry. By and large, these pre-Boom translators rendered Darío into rhymed poems that aimed for fluency above all. This was the conventional approach to translating poetry during the nineteenth century and the beginning of the twentieth. Nearly forty years would go by before another book-length translation of Darío appeared. As suggested earlier, it did so only once the so-called "Boom" took the English-language book market by storm.

Post-Boom Translations of Darío

Deborah Cohn sheds light on the different fates of two mid-twentieth-century translation programs in the United States, the AAUP (American Association of University Presses) and the CIAR (Center of Inter-American Relations), which coincided for several years, though the former ended before the "Boom" received widespread attention. Cohn analyzes the different strategies taken up by the two programs, exposing their motivations and comparing their successes. The result does not only reveal the complex circuitry through which the "Boom" ran its course in the US literary market, but also illuminates the functioning of the literary field at large.

According to Cohn, by publishing translated Latin American authors in university presses, the AAUP laid the groundwork for developing a market for the region's literature. Before the mid-century, Latin American studies was an exiguous academic field; it was unthinkable for something like the AAUP to have existed. Still, despite its relative success, it ultimately was not able to reach a wider readership as it did not capitalize on commercial presses, unlike the CIAR, which took advantage of publishers and translation programs to do so.[107] When comparing the different editions of an author as acclaimed as Borges, she explains the following:

> In contrast [to the CIAR program], literary works published through the AAUP program, where marketing was left to individual UP's, did not fare nearly as well. For the most part, each book only received between one and seven reviews. Even Borges's *Dream Tigers* and *Other Inquisitions, 1937–1952*, both published by the University of Texas Press, only received two and three reviews, respectively, in their first editions. (Both works were later picked up and reissued—with the same translation and copyright—by New York commercial publishers, at which point *Dream Tigers* was reviewed in seven periodicals and *Other Inquisitions, 1937–1952* in five.)[108]

The same university publisher of Borges's scarcely read first editions in English, University of Texas Press, published a collection of Darío's poetry in 1965 called *Selected Poems of Rubén Darío*, translated by Lysander Kemp, also a translator of Octavio Paz, Mario Vargas Llosa, and Juan Rulfo.[109] In other words: almost fifty years after the publication of *Eleven Poems*, the "Boom" of Spanish American literature in translation had come to Darío, albeit through its less popular channel. As mentioned earlier, by then free verse had been consolidated as the conventional poetic idiom and translated books could be read on their own as works of literature proper.[110] Both these changes are clear in Kemp's edition and should be unsurprising given their context. What is surprising is the extent to which this translation again failed to produce any further interest in Darío's writing, since another book-length translation would not be published until 2001, almost forty years afterward.[111]

Now that a small readership for Latin American poetry did exist, why was there no new interest in one of Spanish America's major poets once a new translation was released fifty years after his death? Some of the reasons are likely to be those mentioned earlier, namely the air of outdatedness that Darío's *fin-de-siècle* poetics had, especially among a readership that read Spanish American writers through a modernist and/or Deep Image lens. Also, many of his poetic innovations are language-specific, not least the comprehensive expansion that Spanish-language prosody underwent in his hands. Furthermore, the narrow academic audiences to which these editions were restricted, as Cohn's article convincingly explains, would have only highlighted the distance between Darío's writing and the expectations of a post-war Anglo-American and British readership.

In line with the cultural practices of the Deep Image poets, there was also an expectation of exoticism in the reception of Spanish American literature, on which the publishing industry capitalized. As an example, Munday discusses the reception of García Márquez in the UK, who up until the publication of *El amor en los tiempos del cólera* (1985) was merely depicted as a magical realist writer of fabulous tales, whose Caribbean fictional world was seen as exotic and exciting. Very little was said about his politics or his other works which are not magical realist.[112] The example of García Márquez, arguably the best known of Spanish American writers, is telling of readerly expectations regarding translated literature from the region. The later success of writers such as Roberto Bolaño and César Aira can be explained, too, according to these coordinates. The former's sprawling novels, particularly *Los detectives salvajes* (1998), have an air of adventure to them, something of the road trip novel, as they let the reader travel to many cities of Latin America. The latter's nonsense fiction clearly delivers on the promise of novels that are, if not somewhat magical, exotic by force of their zany absurdism.[113] Furthermore, as seen earlier, these cultural expectations are not restricted to fiction.

If we consider the Parisian setting and the Greco-Roman motifs that abound in Darío's poetry, along with the fact that it is a poetry written in rhymed verse whose tone often has the solemnity which Romantic and post-Romantic poets, convinced of their key role for society, were unabashed to take up—it's easy to see how the Nicaraguan poet would not have met expectations. Lastly, the arguable degree of success of the translations themselves is also likely to have played an important role, though it's worth remembering that if even Borges's works published through the AAUP received scant attention, it's not surprising that Darío failed to cause a stir.

As mentioned previously, it would take almost another forty years for the next publication of a book-length translation of Darío in English, when scholars Will Derusha and Alberto Acereda published their renderings of a large selection of poems under the title *Selected Poems of Rubén Darío: A Bilingual Anthology* (2001). During the first decade of the 2000s, after years of silence, we suddenly see a rapid increase in publications of Darío translations: one year later Stanley Appelbaum published *Stories and Poems/Cuentos y Poesías: A Dual-Language Book* (2002); then Derusha and Acereda published their translation of Darío's *Cantos de vida y esperanza*, rendered as *Songs of Life and Hope* (2004); finally, the translation discussed at the beginning of this chapter, published by Penguin Classics and criticized by González Echevarría, appeared as *Rubén Darío: Selected Writings* (2006). Among the possible reasons for this sudden burst of translations, two in particular seem most likely: on the one hand, the growth of the academic book market as a global market, which includes both Spanish American literature and translation studies as two growing scholarly fields, likely led to the involvement of more academics as translators of Darío. On the other hand, the growth of the Hispanic community in the United States, as well as the consolidation of Latinx and Chicano literature, means that public figures such as Ilan Stavans became capable of mustering enough credibility and prestige for publishers to believe in the existence of a readership for authors like Darío.[114] Nevertheless, Darío is still considerably less familiar to an English-speaking reader than Octavio Paz, Pablo Neruda, Federico García Lorca, César Vallejo, and Jorge Luis Borges. Why?

The Difficulty of Translating Darío

At this point, the extent to which Darío can be translated at all is a question worth addressing. According to Pacheco, "Darío es tan intraducible como Goethe, Pushkin o Yeats. Ni su música verbal ni sus rimas pasan bien a ningún otro idioma."[115] The Mexican author's mention of "música verbal" is not to be taken merely as a figure of speech: the challenge of translating Darío is the challenge of translating prosody. Many of the shortcomings of Darío's translators are in some way related to a failure to render those aural qualities.

In fact, the difficulty of translating the *modernista* is a common trope among his translators, from Muna Lee to Alberto Acereda. Alongside Will Derusha, the latter explains the following:

> Despite his [Darío's] significance as one of the greatest innovators of Hispanic literature, few attempts have been made to translate his works, particularly

his poetry, into English. There are practical reasons for such neglect. The very ingenuity that makes Darío so important also makes him one of the most difficult poets to translate into other languages, in part because of the musicality of his rhyme and rhythm that becomes extravagantly singsong when followed too tightly and sounds curiously flat when not followed closely enough. In addition, much of the original charm of his verse depends on a craftsmanship that has gone out of style in the United States and elsewhere and may sound like affectation to the contemporary ear. The scarcity of solid, representative translations since Darío's death nearly a century ago is probably the best evidence of the difficulty in expressing a real sense of his poetry in English.[116]

In the Penguin edition of Darío mentioned earlier, Greg Simon and Steven F. White include a brief translators' note preceding the poetry section of the collection. As is the case of Derusha and Acereda, Darío's rhymes are a central problem for these translators too. They describe the poems as "formal challenges," "Pythagorean proposals," and "new doorways to the slightly dissonant harmonics of rhyme and slant rhyme in English."[117]

Aside from its near-perfect rhyme, Darío's poetry is thick in connotations: often a choice of word or a turn of phrase will say very little but suggest quite a lot. Upon answering a question about translation, Borges used Darío's word order to show how even translation within the same language is ostensibly impossible.

> Dentro de un mismo idioma la traducción es imposible. Shakespeare es intraducible a otro inglés que no sea el suyo. Imaginemos una traducción literal de un verso de Darío: "La princesa está pálida en su silla de oro" es literalmente igual a "En su silla de oro está pálida la princesa". En el primer caso el verso es muy lindo, ¿no?, por lo menos para los fines musicales que él busca. Su traducción literal, en cambio, no es nada, no existe.[118]

Borges is referring to what is lost when the line goes from an anapestic rhythm to an irregular one. While the literal meaning remains intact, the "music" is somehow gone.

T.S. Eliot writes that "a musical poem" is a poem "which has a musical pattern of sound and a musical pattern of the secondary meanings of the words which compose it, and that these two patterns are indissoluble and one."[119] These secondary meanings to which Eliot makes reference are connotations—an aspect of language whereby the workings of words become increasingly difficult to perceive, as they touch on cultural associations which are not self-evident, at times unconscious, buried in our memory, or all those things at once. For Eliot, a "musical poem" not only has a musical pattern of sound that articulates it, but also another corresponding pattern of secondary meanings (connotations) which together compose it. Our critical vocabulary is clumsy at naming connotations, not only because it requires a skilled reader to identify them, but because they are grounded in cultural identity, which changes over space and time.

The poetry of the *fin de siècle* gave new life to Greco-Roman mythology, was heavily influenced by the esoteric currents of the period, cherished ambiguity and nuance, and cultivated metrical experimentation. The French poet Paul Verlaine, the Italian Gabriele D'Annunzio, the German Stefan Georg, and the Portuguese Eugénio de Castro, just like the Nicaraguan Rubén Darío, wrote a poetry rich in what Eliot calls "a musical pattern of the secondary meanings of the words which compose it." It was not until movements such as Imagism (1914) and Surrealism (1917) came about that imagery came to the fore in poetic creation.

As an imagist himself, Pound put forth an idiosyncratic classification of poetry where he divided it into three types according to the effect words had on the reader. He called the use of words to cast images on the eye of the reader's mind *phanopoeia* (from the Ancient Greek φαίνω, which means "to cause to appear," and ποίησις, which means "poetry" or "creation"), that which ironically plays with linguistic habits, expectations, and conventions, *logopoeia* (λόγος means "word" or "speech"), and the use of words by which they are charged with some musical property that goes beyond their literal meaning *melopoeia*. I mention all of this because *fin-de-siècle* poetry plainly falls in the third category, about which Pound adds with characteristic hyperbole:

> The *melopoeia* can be appreciated by a foreigner with a sensitive ear, even though he be ignorant of the language in which the poem is written. It is practically impossible to transfer or translate it from one language to another, save perhaps by divine accident, and for half a line at a time.[120]

Pound's insistence on the untranslatability of the aural qualities of poetry gives us another point of view on why translations of Darío, an exceptionally "musical" poet, have failed time and again to spur any further interest in his poetry in the English-speaking world.

However, perhaps it's not so much a matter of untranslatability as it is of an inadequacy of our own translation practices when it comes to rendering those aural qualities along with their connotations. As Venuti explains, behind every translation strategy there is an implicit theory of language based on which its choices are made, whether the translator is aware of it or not. So-called "domestication," for instance, which Venuti conceives as underpinned by the desire to achieve fluency at the expense of other aspects of the source text, tends to assume a theory of language as communication, in which immediate intelligibility is the priority and both polysemy and ambiguities are to be avoided. Words are conceived as carriers of meaning, the latter of which is often considered something literal and shared by all languages, albeit in different ways.[121] This is arguably the same theory of language that underpins inventions such as the dictionary and Roget's Thesaurus.

It would be outrageous to claim that dictionaries are simply wrong, or that literal meaning is not something that languages share—yet literal meaning is only the first or primary meaning of a word. The connotations of a word or grouping of words are its deeper meanings. According to the *OED*, etymologically the word "denote" has its roots in the late sixteenth century; the prefix "de" meant "away, or thoroughly" and "notare," in turn, "to observe, to note." Therefore, the French *dénoter* or the Latin *denotare* meant "to be a sign of, to mark out." Likewise, the prefix "con" in "connote" meant "together with"; the Latin *connotare* meant "to mark in addition." Words mark something, or are a sign of it, and that is their denotation; at the same time, they point toward something other, and those are their connotations. But the latter are fickle, culturally and historically bound, sometimes even unwieldy, and therefore difficult to put down in print in a way that would make them unanimous for all users of a language. Lexicographers can leave them untouched, yet translators—especially translators of poetry—cannot afford that luxury.

And yet, most of Darío's recent translators, while aware of the exacting nuances of his poetry, seem to overlook the complexities of translation. In his introduction, Appelbaum briefly describes the criteria of his edition as follows:

> In addition to providing an accurate, "no-frills" translation (line-for-line in the poetry section) in modern American English (but striving to match the lexical level of the Spanish at all points), the present translator's biggest task was to identify the best Spanish texts of the items selected.[122]

He also comments on the many inconsistencies and poor quality of the editions of Darío in Spanish. Though the passage above would seem to communicate very little about the author's ideas on translation, the paucity of Appelbaum's description is telling. Elsewhere he describes Darío's poetry from *Prosas profanas* in the following terms:

> In *Prosas profanas*, Darío is at his most extravagantly innovative, with recherché vocabulary, ethereally beautiful versification, and wide-ranging thought. To many, this volume is the summit of his achievement, and of modernismo in general.[123]

Ironically, the "accurate" rendering of a writer who shares the characteristics mentioned above would pose formidable challenges to any translator. However, Appelbaum seems to imply in the passage cited previously that, when the conditions of "accuracy" and "lexical matching" are met, the real question for a translator lies only in the selection of texts. A striking undervaluation of the complexity of how words create the effects he mentions—extravagant innovation, recherché vocabulary, ethereal beauty, and so forth—is at play here. The translator's implied theory of language seems to be relatively simple: if the literal meaning of words is rendered, the rest will follow.

Despite the ingenuousness of the account, Appelbaum is reacting here as a literary scholar to the unwarranted liberties taken by early twentieth-century translators of Darío who, as we saw previously, prioritized rhyme at the expense of all other features of the poem. This is also the case of Derusha and Acereda. Just as Appelbaum underlines the "accuracy" of his versions, Derusha and Acereda do so regarding the "fidelity" of theirs:

> It is our hope that scholars will again appreciate the fidelity to the Spanish originals, while the careful rendering of the verses in English will find a ready public among teachers, students, and lovers of poetry.
>
> Our own experience in reading Spanish poetry in English translation has generally been frustrating in terms of meaning, rhythm, and grammatical construction. In teaching Spanish poetry in translation, we have often confronted texts that baffle and discourage students and, very likely, the majority of nonspecialists. We value a text that imparts some real sense of the original poetic voice in its own time and place, rather than a sense of the translator.[124]

What's problematic here is the notion that fidelity alone leads to "some real sense of the original poetic voice in its own time and place, rather than a sense of the translator." Despite forgoing rhyme, the authors later claim to have translated "much of the structural and acoustic dimensions of [Darío's] language."[125] But it's difficult to imagine how to render a *modernista* poem's structural and prosodic dimensions without some kind of rhyme. For a poet such as Darío, rhyme is not only his poetic idiom, but a determining factor in the way the poem is composed.

In contrast, perhaps owing to the nature of their edition and its appeal to a wider audience, Simon and White have a more liberal take on translating Darío for the Penguin Classic series, to the extent of claiming to have abandoned a purely rational approach and in its stead having embraced a more subjective one, quoting Douglas Robinson's words: "humans translate truly, restoratively, only when they hear and become a responsive part of the translating of spirit."[126] As pointed out by González Echevarría, the result shows many mistranslations and instances of gauche "translatese."

In the end, due to its emphasis on what Darío calls *(h)armonía* and *melodía*, the main qualities of his poetry comprise all the things with which our long-standing translation practices have struggled to grapple: prosody, ambiguity, connotation. Darío's oeuvre is not alone in this sense, and one could add the same names as Pacheco in his quote cited earlier. However, as suggested previously, the difference is that, unlike Goethe, Yeats, and Pushkin, Darío, whose stature within his language is roughly analogous to the German, Irish, and Russian examples, is still very much unknown among English-speaking readers.

A Closer Look at the Translations

"Canto de esperanza" and "¡Torres de Dios!...", from *Cantos de vida y esperanza*, are two poems which appear in five of the book-length translations mentioned so far. That is to say, Salomón de la Selva, Greg Simon and Steven White, Lysander Kemp, Will Derusha and Alberto Acereda, and Stanley Appelbaum have all rendered them in their own way. It's worth looking at their versions briefly, if only to sketch out translation patterns and identify meaningful divergences among them. To close this chapter, this comparative reading will help us to understand how translators have rendered Darío over the years and give us a bird's-eye view of the different tendencies in doing so.

Below are the first two stanzas from the original Spanish of "Canto de Esperanza":

Canto de esperanza

Un gran vuelo de cuervos mancha el azul celeste.
Un soplo milenario trae amagos de peste.
Se asesinan los hombres en el extremo Este.

¿Ha nacido el apocalíptico Anticristo?
Se han sabido presagios y prodigios se han visto
y parece inminente el retorno del Cristo. (ll. 1–6)

The lines are single-rhymed Alexandrines, whose triadic rhythm gives a sense of unity to each stanza and strings them together as the poem unfolds. Here are the renderings of those translators who, for the most part, opt for rhyme in irregular pentameter:

Song of Hope (*de la Selva*)

Vultures a-wing have sullied the glory of the sky;

The winds bear on their opinions the horror of Death's cry;

Assassining [*sic*] one another, men rage and fall and die.

Song of Hope (*Simon & White*)

A great flock of crows is staining the sky.

The winds of millennial plagues blow by.

In the far eastern war, many men die.

Song of Hope (*de la Selva*)	Song of Hope (*Simon & White*)
Has Antichrist arisen whom John at Patmos saw?	Is this a sign of the Antichrist's birth?
Portents are seen and marvels that fill the world with awe,	Apocalyptic omens of the earth
And Christ's return seems pressing, coming to fulfil the Law.	that foreshadow Christ's imminent return?

In the first case, de la Selva must take liberties to preserve the rhyme in, albeit quite irregular, pentameter. He misses out on the powerful imagery of the first line: "un gran vuelo de cuervos mancha el azul celeste" suggests the image of an ink stain blotting the sky. The fact that they are crows in the source text, and not vultures, is important: the connotations that crows conjure have to do with the color black and bad omens, while vultures as birds of prey suggest other meanings related to death. Likewise, the omission of a flock undoes the power of the image, as the reader needs the flock for the birds to seem, at a distance, like a single blot of ink. There is an added emphasis on the glory of the sky, too, in the English version. Imagery and tone come across as somewhat more pious here than in the original.

The second line is overwrought: where Darío creates an apocalyptic atmosphere through the image of a millennial wind, the translator personifies the wind as carrier of the horror of Death's cry. The line is now less about an apocalyptic omen than about the wind as a metaphysical force of death. As said previously, the translator must take liberties if they are to preserve the rhyme; however, in doing so, he has let some of the more powerful features of these initial lines go to waste.

The strange use of "assassining" (not "assassinating," as standard English would have it) in line three is worth at least a passing comment. The wording could be explained by an interference of Spanish in de la Selva's hand at work: the Spanish word *asesinar* might have led the translator to write "assassinating" as "assassining." This might be an indication of de la Selva's uncertain command of English verse mentioned earlier.

By contrast, Simon and White's translation is more successful: it's straightforward like the original and manages to preserve the powerful imagery of the first line, as well as the rhyme for the first stanza. However, because the penultimate line scans one or two feet short, it fails to keep the rhythm and rhyme at the end of the second stanza, despite going as far as recasting the last two lines in the form of a question.

Below is Kemp's rendering.

Song of Hope (*Kemp*)

A great flock of crows defiles the heavenly blue.
A millennial blast of wind brings threats of pestilence.
Men are being murdered in the Far East.

Has the apocalyptic Antichrist been born?
There have been omens, there have been prodigal sights,
and it would appear the return of Christ is at hand.

Kemp translates into free verse, seeking a balance between a certain proximity to the original and an up-to-date poetic idiom in English. However, the latter sometimes elevates Darío's language when it does not require it. In the first line, the flock of crows "defiles," not "stains," the heavenly blue. As in de la Selva's rendering, the translator misses out on the powerful imagery of the original. There are also stronger biblical overtones in the use of anaphora in line five, rendering the prophetic tone of the lines slightly more solemn and grave, which is also meant to compensate for rhythm.

It's worth mentioning that Kemp's collection of translations is the only book not to have the Spanish originals facing his own renderings of the poems: Unlike Darío's later translators, Kemp's book aspires to be read as a literary text on its own and not a study aid. This sheds light on the context in which the translation was published. As mentioned earlier, Anglo-American and British Modernism had cleared the way for translation as an autonomous genre—and Kemp is a poet, not a scholar.

Derusha/Acereda's and Appelbaum's translations, as discussed earlier, render these stanzas more or less literally:

Song of Hope (*Derusha & Acereda*)
A great flight of crows sullies the
celestial blue.
A millennial gust of wind smacks
of pestilence.
Men are killing each other in the
Far East.

Has the apocalyptic Antichrist
been born?
Omens have been discovered and
prodigies seen,
and the return of Christ seems
imminent.

Song of Hope (*Appelbaum*)
A long flight of crows blots the blue
of the sky.
A wind from the gulf of ages is
bearing signs of plague.
Men are being murdered in the
Far East.

Has the Antichrist of the
Apocalypse been born?
Omens have been learned of, and
wonders have been seen,
and the return of the Christ seems
imminent.

Forgoing the poem's rhymes, Derusha and Acereda follow Darío's Spanish syntax closely, while aiming to render it into natural English. On the other hand, Appelbaum is the only one to grasp the importance of the imagery of the first line, even if he seems to convey elongated ink stains in his choice of "a long flight of crows." Interestingly, he resorts to repetition on the same line as Kemp did (l. 5), while aiming to render a straightforward translation of the Spanish. While neither of these translators preserves rhyme in their rendering, Derusha and Acereda maintain a pentameter throughout.

To see how consistent these strategies are, let's move on to the second poem. Here are the first two stanzas of "¡Torres de Dios! ... " in the original Spanish.

Torres de Dios! [sic]

Torres de Dios! Poetas! [sic]
Pararrayos celestes,
que resistís las duras tempestades,
como crestas escuetas,
como picos agrestes,
rompeolas de las eternidades!

La mágica Esperanza anuncia un día
en que sobre la roca de armonía

expirará la pérfida sirena.
Esperad, esperemos todavía! (ll. 1-9)

The irregular meter of the poem makes it even more difficult to translate into rhymed verse. Below are the two rhymed translations:

Towers of God! Poets! (*de la Selva*)	Towers of God! Poets! (*Simon & White*)
Made to resist the fury of the storms	You bear the storms that are infernal
Like cliffs beside the ocean	like a jagged mountain range,
Or clouded, savage peaks!	like a heavenly lightning rod,
Masters of lightning!	breakwaters of the eternal,
Like Breakwaters of eternity!	high summits that will never change!
Hope, magic-voiced, foretells the day	Hope with its magic announces the day
When on the rock of harmony	when, thrown against the shoals of harmony,
The Siren traitorous shall die and pass away,	the treacherous mermaid will pass away.
And there shall only be	But wait, and don't lose your patience with me!
The full, frank-billowed music of the sea.	

We can see here how editorial carelessness leads to unintended divergences among translations. Both these renderings construe the first line "Torres de Dios! Poetas!" as merely the title of the poem, while the title is actually "Torres de Dios!". Already we can appreciate the philological value of Derusha and Acereda's edition of the book, which is one of the most rigorous to date.[127] Besides this, it's understandable that the translators rearrange the lines if they are to successfully complete their rhymes. De la Selva displaces line two in the original ("Pararrayos celestes") to line four, while Simon and White do likewise onto line three. The former translator also expands the second stanza by adding a line that helps him complete the rhyme; however, he seems to have been unable to rhyme the first stanza.

However, de la Selva completely changes line nine, which preserves no resemblance to the original and arguably takes the poem in another direction, both thematically and tonally, giving greater significance to the sea and its frank-billowed music. In turn, Simon and White have changed some of the poem's allusions and added distorting connotations. Unlike the original, where poets are said to endure "duras tempestades," in this rendering poets bear storms that are infernal—a description whose religious overtones should be carefully weighed in the case of Darío, some of whose main themes are religious doubt and the tension between paganism and Catholicism. They also write "mermaids" where the original Spanish has "sirena," in allusion to Homeric sirens and not the woman-cum-fish of European folk. This change of wording risks changing the poem's depiction of the poet's plight as a journey not unlike that of Odysseus. As in many *fin-de-siècle* poets, this is a recurrent trope in Darío and therefore an important one.

Below is Kemp's rendition.

Towers of God! Poets! (*Kemp*)

Towers of God! Poets!
Lightning rods of Heaven
that resist the fierce storms
like solitary mountains,
like peaks in the wilderness!
Breakwaters of eternity!

Magic hope foretells
the day when the traitorous siren
will die on her musical rock.
Hope! Let us still hope!

Unlike the translators of rhyme, thanks to free verse Kemp does not need to rearrange lines, though as a result he loses the poem's music. The rendering is all in all a solid one, even if "like solitary mountains" (l. 4) is a flat rendering of "como crestas escuetas."

Finally, here are the literal translations of the beginning of the poem.

Towers of God! Poets! (*Derusha & Acereda*)	Towers of God! Poets! (*Appelbaum*)
Heavenly lightning rods	Heavenly lighting rods
withstanding severe tempests,	that withstand heavy storms,
like unadorned crests,	like bare mountain crests,
like rustic peaks,	like wild peaks,
breakwaters of eternities!	breakwaters of eternity!
Magical Hope announces the day	Magical hope proclaims a day
when on the rock of harmony	when, on her musical rock,
the perfidious siren will pass away.	the treacherous siren will perish.
You must have hope, let's still hope!	Hope! Let us keep hoping!

As before, both translations are close to the original when it comes to syntax and semantic meaning, and therefore offer similar results. Unlike the previous example, however, Derusha and Acereda manage to slip in one rhyme in the second strophe. Notoriously, none of these translators decides to reproduce the ambiguity of the line "¡Esperad, esperemos todavía!" (l. 9) either, in which "esperar" does not exactly mean plain hope but rather a hopeful wait for change, an expectation.

Though some of these renderings are fair translations, these examples show mistranslations and lacks which also appeared in the versions analyzed previously. Altogether, they display the effect the poetic norms of a period have on the manner in which a text tends to be translated: de la Selva, like Muna Lee, Alice Blackwell, and Dundas Craig, prioritizes rhyme in his renderings. By contrast, Kemp, a mid-twentieth century US poet and translator, renders Darío intro free verse and in standalone versions which do away with a facing source text. Likewise, recent Darío translators who also happen to be scholars, such as Appelbaum, Derusha, and Acereda, translate his writing into free verse that prioritizes semantic fidelity to the text. Readership also plays an important role: Simon and White's versions done for the Penguin edition, which is intended for a wide audience, are rhymed and free in manner. It goes without saying that none of these translators is successful in recreating the richness of Darío's prosody, which is at the heart of his writing.

However, the reason behind the paucity of translations of Rubén Darío's writing goes well beyond the linguistic; it entails understanding the developments of the two literary cultures involved. As already mentioned, his poetry is extremely challenging to translate. Translated poetry in English as a genre has struggled to render the aural qualities which are essential to the writing of poets from Darío's time. However, because his poetry was so heavily invested in a dialogue with the literature of his time, the outdatedness of many of the values espoused by him, and those of many of his interlocutors—namely the Parnassians and Pre-Raphaelites—belong to the Anglo-American and British nineteenth century. By the middle twentieth century, merely three decades after his death, Darío's modernity had already stopped being modern. There seems to be little there for the modernists, or the Deep Image poets later, to have become interested in.

On the other hand, the scarcity of translations also reflects the English-speaking world's lack of interest in Latin American literature and culture before the 1960s. Though he was often published in both English and Spanish-language periodicals in the United States, these reached only a limited audience. Moreover, whenever he appeared in translation anthologies from as early as the 1930s, he was presented as literary history: However great and innovative a poet, he is only the background of the truly exciting and contemporary poetry being written at the time.

If we focus on the second half of the twentieth century, given the pictures of Spanish American literature fashioned by the Deep Image movement and the "Boom," the persistent scarcity of translations of his work reflects English-speaking preconceptions of what Latin American poetry looks like: experimental, exotic, masculine, magical, or otherwise. Darío fits into none of those categories. The scholarly rescue of Darío's writing has led to important philological work, such as Derusha and Acereda's edition of *Songs of Life and Hope*. Nevertheless, these translators grossly overestimate the capacity of literal renderings to convey a sense of original poems in which prosody is so important. Likewise, they underestimate the complexities of translation and its covert interplay with reading practices. While scholarly renderings can indeed help works circulate among universities—which in turn can help to safekeep a body of work that has otherwise been edited with dubious care—as in the case of periodicals, they do little to find a wider audience for a writer.

Coda: Translating Darío's Poetics of (H)armonía

In his best-known poems and in the prefaces to his poetry collections, Darío elaborated on the importance that rhythm had for his writing. In "Palabras liminares," the preface to *Prosas profanas y otros poemas* (1896), we find the following passage:

> ¿Y la cuestión métrica? ¿Y el ritmo?
> Como cada palabra tiene un alma, hay en cada verso, además de la harmonía [*sic*] verbal, una melodía ideal. La música es sólo de la idea, muchas veces.[1]

Darío would later echo these thoughts in his preface to *El canto errante* (1907), "Dilucidaciones":

> He, sí, cantado aires antiguos; y he querido ir hacia el porvenir, siempre bajo el divino imperio de la música—música de las ideas, música del verbo [...] el arte no es un conjunto de reglas, sino una armonía de caprichos [...] Hay una música ideal como hay una música verbal.[2]

Much has been written about the role that the modest genre of the preface had for *Modernismo* and particularly for Darío, who often wrote his own like prose poems, using them not only to elaborate on his poetics, but to provoke and criticize his fellow writers and readers. Among the scholarship on the topic, Guillermo Sucre has commented on the passage quoted previously from "Palabras liminares." According to the Venezuelan writer, when Darío states "la música es sólo de la idea" he is defining music not only as a system of sounds, but more widely as one of relations or correspondences. For Darío, musicality has a twofold nature; on the one hand, it is sensitive insofar as it pertains to the musicality of words, which is perceived through the senses; on the other, it is ideal or ideational insofar as the ideas that those musical words put forth can correspond with each other harmoniously on a conceptual level. The use of musicality in *Modernismo* is thus predicated upon a whole rhythmic system of correspondences that works on both a conceptual and a verbal level.[3]

This "música ideal" that also appears in the preface to *El canto errante* has its roots in an esoteric view of the world that can be traced back to Pythagoras, at which Darío arrived through the writings of prominent occultists such as Josephin Péladan and Éduoard Schuré. In his classic essay on Darío, "El caracol y la sirena" (1964), Octavio Paz touched on the place of the occult in Darío's poetry, leading the way for the research of scholars such as Raymond Skyrme's *Rubén Darío and the Pythagorean Tradition* (1975) and Cathy L. Jade's *Rubén Darío and the Romantic Search for Unity* (1983). Both studies consider the extent to which Darío's worldview and poetics were intimately joined at the idea of "armonía." Jrade explains how occult beliefs on the one hand—a mélange of Pythagoreanism, Platonism, and Neoplatonism, as found in Schuré's *Les grands initiés* (1889)—and Romantic and Symbolist writings on the other, led Darío to develop "a poetic cosmology,"[4] according to which the poet's calling is to interpret the harmonious order of the universe. For the *modernista* there is a sacred correspondence in the universe which, following Pythagoras's putative teachings, arises from the ratio that musical scales and the celestial spheres share. This was hardly original on the part of Darío, as there are ample examples of such beliefs in the writings of Nerval, Hugo, and Baudelaire, to name some of the best-known French cases.[5] In his study, Skyrme elaborates on how this belief in the harmony of all things applies to Darío's poetics, not only in the obvious sense that words should create harmony through their mellifluous sound, but also be semantically interconnected (hence "música de la idea"):

> Words carry with them clusters of associations, which the poet, through the sound, rhythm, and disposition of the words in a given utterance, seeks to call upon the reader's mind. The semantic interrelationship of the words, reinforced by sound and rhythm, becomes the ordering force within the poem and creates its unity.[6]

Similarly, Sucre touches on this concept in Darío's poetry, relating it to rhythm and quoting the many instances in which the word "(h)armonía" occurs in the Nicaraguan's poetry: "El Hada Harmonía ritmaba sus vuelos," we read in the first poem of *Prosas profanas*. In a later poem published two decades afterwards in *El canto errante*, we read: "El canto vuela, con sus alas: / Armonía y Eternidad" in the manner of an *ars poetica*. The examples abound. For Darío's poetics, "armonía" is the most important principle.[7]

Alberto Julián Pérez expands on what "armonía" implies in specifically poetic terms, tracing its presence in some of Darío's well-known poems. The passage is worth quoting in full for its sweep:

> La armonía es uno de los conceptos "musicales" relevantes que Darío repite con más frecuencia en su poesía: en "Era un aire suave ... " ("el hada harmonía ritmaba sus vuelos"), "El país del Sol" ("hermana harmoniosa"), "Responso" a Verlaine ("la harmonía sideral"), "Yo soy aquél" (" ... trajo de/ la sagrada selva la armonía"), etc. [...] Darío no usa la palabra en sentido puramente musical: se refiere a un ideal poético, literario, que considera a la armonía una variedad de sonidos, medidas y pausas bien concertadas y gratas. [...] Darío creía en la armonización de la palabra y la idea, en la armonización del yo poético con la existencia espiritual del todo, la divinidad [...] Su búsqueda de armonía (el equilibrio concertado en la totalidad del poema, valiéndose del ritmo, de la melodía, de la asimilación de sonidos vocálicos) es inseparable de su concepción poética idealista metafísica.[8]

Pérez underlines the importance of musical or acoustic qualities in the poetry of Darío—"ritmo," "melodía," "sonidos vocálicos"—which are all related to his notion of "armonía." In turn, other scholars have taken these acoustic qualities as a starting point for their interpretation of Darío's writing in particular and of *Modernismo* in general: Noé Jitrik's *Las contradicciones del modernismo* (1978) and Erika Lorenz's *Bajo el divino imperio de la música* (1956) are two examples of this approach.[9]

The poems themselves serve as the best illustration of this aspect of Darío's poetics. Among those added to the second edition of *Prosas profanas* (1901), many under the section "Las ánforas de Epicuro" can be read as metapoetic sonnets. In these texts the metaphors for poetry are always musical, following Darío's esoteric conception of harmony. The clearest example of this can be found in "Ama tu ritmo":

> Ama tu ritmo y ritma tus acciones
> bajo su ley, así como tus versos;
> eres un universo de universos
> y tu alma es una fuente de canciones.
>
> La celeste unidad que presupones
> hará brotar de ti mundos diversos,
> y al resonar tus números dispersos
> pitagoriza en tus constelaciones.
>
> Escucha la retórica divina
> del pájaro del aire y la nocturna
> irradiación geométrica adivina;
>
> mata la indiferencia taciturna
> y engarza perla y perla cristalina
> en donde la verdad vuelca su urna.[10]

All aspects of Darío's poetry and beliefs discussed so far are articulated in this sonnet where ethics and aesthetics come together: poetry is song and rhythm; the poet must shape his actions after that rhythm; and he should do so by listening to the music of the universe without, discovering the universe within. From the first to the last line, sound and sense are tightly interwoven. The hendecasyllables written with feminine rhymes abound in assonance, internal rhyme, and an ingenious use of repetition in a way that performs the very meaning of the poem. In other words, through the text of the sonnet Darío "[ritma] sus acciones," shows himself to be "una fuente de canciones," which the reader can find in his "universo de universos," and so on.

What happens to a poem like "Ama tu ritmo" when it is translated with no consideration to prosody? Here is Appelbaum's almost word-for-word translation.

> Love your rhythm and rhythm your actions
> in obedience to its law, and your poetry as well;
> you are a universe of universes,
> and your soul a fountain of song.
>
> The celestial unity that you presuppose
> will make varied worlds germinate within you,

and as your scattered poems resound,
philosophize like Pythagoras among your constellations.

Listen to the divine rhetoric
of the bird in the air, and divine
the geometric radiation of the night;

slay silent indifference
and string pearl on crystalline pearl
there where truth pours out her urn. (131)

Suddenly, all the aural qualities of the poem which are crucial for it to fulfill its meaning as an *ars poetica* are absent. The unity between sense and sound—its "armonía"—is broken.

Joan Boase-Beier calls that point in every poem where translators consistently diverge from the source text the "eye of the poem"—that is, the poem's critical point. She explains that

> The eye of the poem, then, is a crucial point in the poem, which both expresses the poem's vision and allows the reader access to the cognitive state informing the poem. In stylistic terms, I would suggest that the eye of the poem is recognisable by, firstly, a maximum of foregrounding, that is, of linguistic structures which are "made prominent" [...] and which, metaphorically speaking, attract the eye of the reader, and, secondly, by ambiguity, which allows the poem to be read in at least two different ways.[11]

Despite issues of its applicability as a concept to different styles of poetry (and how it's likely to vary from language to language) the concept of the eye of a poem is an interesting one to put to the test when looking at the renderings of Darío's works. It can help us identify passages of a text where translators consistently diverge because of their struggle to render it. It can also be a useful tool to identify overarching patterns that emerge in similar translation strategies applied to the same text. Regarding Appelbaum's "Love Your Rhythm ...," the eye of the poem seems to be at the end of the sonnet's octave, where

y al resonar tus números dispersos
pitagoriza en tus constelaciones (ll. 7–8)

is rendered as

> and as your scattered poems resound
> philosophize like Pythagoras among your constellations. (ll. 7–8)

The choice to render "pitagoriza" by expanding on an interpretation of the neologism ("philosophize like Pythagoras") is telling: the facing English version is almost meant to decode the Spanish text for the student who reads it. And yet it's still not clear what exactly "philosophize like Pythagoras" means. Without further information, it's as ambiguous as the verb "pitagoriza"—which, given Darío's occultist beliefs, is likely meant to exhort the reader to find harmony between the self and the universe. Choosing to preserve the neologism in English ("pythagorize") would have been easier, not to mention that it would not have disrupted the line's rhythm and length. Since sound and sense are so closely bound throughout the poem, Appelbaum is forced to rewrite the lines. As a result, the meaning changes slightly, and the rhythm of the poem seems to stagger in the last line of the quatrain.

As I said before, the harmony that the source text possesses conceptually ("música ideal") and prosodically ("música verbal") has been broken. It's not outrageous, therefore, to claim that the translated poem is incomplete, even if it's a somewhat accurate rendering of the literal meaning of the source text. I say this because what is at the heart of "Ama tu ritmo" is the performance of its message of musicality; the poem practices what it preaches. Not all Darío poems perform their message like this one does; however, they all are predicated on the same ideas about poetry and rhythm.

As mentioned earlier, the challenge of translating Darío often comes down to the challenge of translating prosody. Matching the lexical level of the text is not enough to convey the meaning of "Ama tu ritmo," which largely resides in its sound. In this regard, the extent to which Appelbaum's translation reveals how the meaning of a poem by Darío is dependent on his poetics of "armonía" is striking. Anderson Imbert saw this clearly:

> Sin tal melodía, los paisajes y escenografías de Darío hubieran sido convencionales: el oro, el lirio, el cisne y la mujer; el lago en el jardín y el palacio en la ciudad; los objetos de arte, las alhajas y los vestidos suntuosos;

el desfile de figuras míticas, etc. tenían algo de lienzo de fotógrafo o tramoya de teatro. Hubieran perjudicado irremediablemente su obra de no ser por esa música de la idea, que lo envolvía todo en ondas de emoción a un mismo tiempo nostálgicas y anhelantes.[12]

Because the work of a poet is a work upon language, merely translating the dictionary meaning of the words is rarely enough.

To translate "Ama tu ritmo" as fully as possible, the prosody of the lines must come first as we try to follow the ideas of this *ars poetica* as closely as possible. Below is my own rendering of the octave:

> Cherish your rhythm and rhythm
> your actions along, as your verses;
> you are a universe of universes,
> and your soul a many-colored prism.
>
> Inside you there are scintillations
> surrounding buried planets within;
> make your hidden numbers ring
> and pythagorize your constellations. (ll. 1-8)

I have translated neither the "letter" nor the "spirit." Indeed, there are important lexical differences between my rendering and the source text, particularly in lines 4-7. That is because I give preference to the prosodic and figurative qualities of the lines, which are more important for the poem's meaning and effect. Besides translating into rhyme, I render both the musical and astronomical motifs which come together in the celestial picture of the poet's inner voice. Since much of the initial verve of the poem seems to come from the deft play between "ritmo" and "ritma" as noun and verb, as well as in the rich rhyme between "versos" and "universo de universos"—though, alas, I lose the play with "diversos"—it seemed crucial to keep them in my version. As mentioned earlier, I find no reason not to keep the neologism "pitagoriza," a word which brings together the poet's verbal ingenuity and his esoteric purview of the role of poetry in the world. I should also stress that my rendering is not a "free" version of the poem, despite the apparent liberties I take, nor does it oppose other kinds of "faithful" translation. If it were free, I would take Darío's poem into a more interesting direction from a contemporary point of view. I would have discarded the rhyme or at least added a shade of irony to it. Instead, I hew close to the source as far as its "armonía" goes.

Imitating what the sestet says, as well as how it says it, proved to be more challenging. Below is my rendering of the last lines of the sonnet.

> Open your ears and listen
> to the rhetoric of the bird of the air.
> See night's geometry glisten;
>
> slay apathy's quiet heir
> and in joining pearl with pearl fair,
> truth, like a sun, will have risen. (ll. 9-14)

Since Modernism brought about its revolution of free verse, imagery and direct speech have come to the fore in English poetic idiom. Hence, when rendering the lines above, the best choice is to further their imagistic possibilities given the opportunity they offer. For that reason, "la nocturna / irradiación geométrica adivina" becomes "See night's geometry glisten." Given English-language poetics, on the one hand it is unsurprisingly more economical and direct; on the other, it gives Darío's line another kind of visual power while achieving the rhyme that is crucial for the poem's harmony. The last tercet diverges further (semantically) from the source text: "mata la indiferencia taciturna" becomes "slay apathy's quiet heir." Still, the homophony between "air" and "heir" is a way of playing with English that is, in its own way, Daríoesque, and therefore a compensation in place. I would argue that it fits fully with the theme and aim of the *ars poetica*.

For the last two lines, the tension that is created by the repetition of line 13, which in turn culminates in the poet's arrival to truth in line 14, seemed to be the most important features to achieve, while keeping the rhymes without which the spell of the poem would be broken. Thus, "y engarza perla y perla cristalina / en donde la verdad vuelca su urna" is imitated as "and in joining pearl with pearl fair / truth, like a sun, will have risen." Line 13 is rendered in a reasonably successful manner by following the repetition and achieving the full rhyme with a hyperbaton; however, line 14 is decidedly a lesser line of poetry than Darío's. It does not replicate the rich associations that "urna" conjures, both a vase and an urn, and the contents of which are nothing less than truth itself. My ending, on the other hand, borders on the commonplace. Still, it gets the job done by giving the reader an image of culmination with the sun that rises at the end of the poet's long Pythagorean journey of inner discovery, while conveying that such journey leads to truth, which is key for the meaning of the *ars poetica*. It also provides an imaginative half rhyme that chimes with the two lines that appear previously in the poem (listen-glisten-risen) giving a sense of completeness to the poem on a formal level.

This exercise in translation shows how being familiar with a writer's poetics can inform our decisions when somewhat drastic compromises are called for. In my "Cherish your rhythm," some things are lost and some gained when compared to its source text; but it is a poem that successfully puts the *ars poetica* into practice as much as it also preaches it. It also has harmony, in Darío's sense, and aims to convey the Nicaraguan poet's prosodic ingenuity as well as his musical and esoteric motifs.

Conclusion

The foregoing pages show how rethinking a canonical body of work, such as Darío's, from the point of view of another language and tradition can reveal traits or patterns that have remained overlooked, such as the multilingualism of Darío's poetry. They also illustrate how translation can be used as a tool to reread, rethink, and re-present an author's work.

As discussed in Chapter 1, Darío wanted to become a French-language writer. Over the course of his lifelong engagement with French language and literature, he not only wrote poems in French, but translated, glossed, rewrote, annotated, and expanded on other French authors in his own writing. This filled his writing with echoes of French in the shape of Gallicisms, allusions, tropes, motifs, and poetic forms. The true extent of this engagement with his sources has been underestimated, given the narrow notions of literary influence and imitation which Darío scholars have applied to their readings. Likewise, as discussed in Chapter 2, Darío incorporated echoes of Provençal, Latin, Catalan, and early modern Spanish, as part of his wide-ranging *modernista* project of stylistic renewal of literature in Spanish. The image of Darío that emerges thereof is less that of the inspired genius in the ivory tower of *Modernismo*, and more that of an ambitious, toiling, erring, and studious autodidact who conceived literature as something multilingual and transnational. We can now picture the *modernista* working on his poems surrounded by the various texts and images to which they allude.

Translation as a critical tool also sheds light on historical issues: how authors are translated changes historically, as does how they are read. While traditional accounts of translation would suggest that it's mostly a linguistic affair, the discussion in Chapter 3 proves that historical and cultural differences bear on it more heavily. The case of Darío is striking because the history of the translation of his writing holds up a mirror to the history of the translation of Spanish American literature more generally.

As discussed in Chapter 3, the study of the *modernista*'s afterlife in English takes us through the history of Spanish American literature in that language: from the paucity of the first half of the twentieth century, including the Pan-American experiments and Good Neighbor publications, to the turning point the Cuban Revolution represented; from the Deep Image appropriative translations to the so-called "Boom" of Spanish American literature, and from the widespread academization of its study in the decades that followed on to the present. The dearth of interest in Spanish American literature which existed in the Anglophone world before the Cuban Revolution made the reception of Darío extremely unlikely, despite the effort of some maverick translators. In addition, the rise of Modernism rendered his modernity decidedly less modern. Afterward, once the "Boom" was at its zenith, the exoticism which was popularized by the success of magical realist writings, in addition to the postcolonial turn in literature, created readerly expectations regarding Spanish American literature which Darío's writing did not meet. Because of Darío's extremely skillful use of rhythm and rhyme, translators mostly failed to produce compelling renderings of his poetry.

Reading through translation, it also becomes clear how Darío's poetics of *(h)armonía* is not limited to the level of beliefs—Pythagorean, occult, or otherwise—nor to stylistic ornament: His whole poetic system is predicated upon it. Proof of this is that, by applying Daríoesque notions of harmony to the rendering of his poems, one arrives to versions that elicit similar effects as their originals—or at least comes much closer in doing so.

Having a new and more accomplished translation of Darío may help to expand the understanding of the history of Spanish American literature in the Anglophone world. It could also open the door to the translation of other poets who have so far remained in the shadows. By adding a crucial piece that has been missing from the puzzle of Spanish American poetry in English, it could illuminate the context and work of *posmodernistas* and *vanguardistas* that came after the Nicaraguan poet, contributing to undo exoticizing tendencies in the reception of Spanish American literature and help to reshape reader expectations. More effective translations of other *fin-de-siècle* poets such as

Paul Verlaine, Gabriele D'Annunzio, and Stefan George would decisively improve our understanding of modern poetry before Modernism.

What remains for Darío's afterlife in English? Has his time to be translated into English passed? As argued in Chapter 3, it seems that such a time never existed. Today, however, thanks to the increasing importance translated literature has in the Anglophone literary market—alongside a post-boom understanding of Spanish American literature and a post-modernism understanding of modernity—the conditions seem more favorable to new translations of Darío. Aside from my own renderings, which follow the principles laid out in the Coda and which I hope to publish soon, there is reason to be optimistic: As I write these concluding lines, Adam Feinstein, a biographer of Pablo Neruda, has just published new rhymed translations of Darío; and the Latinx poet and translator Francisco Aragón's book *After Rubén* (2020) includes several versions of the *modernista* poet.

Notes

Introduction

1. Pedro Henríquez Ureña, *Literary Currents in Hispanic America* (Cambridge, MA: Harvard University Press, 1945), 169.
2. Peter France, *The Oxford Guide to Literature in English Translation* (Oxford: Oxford University Press, 2000), 431.
3. Ibid.
4. Tom Boll, "Penguin Books and the Translation of Spanish and Latin American Poetry, 1956–1979," *Translation & Literature*, vol. 25, no. 1 (2016), 28–57 (56). Boll provides dates for each edition: Lorca (1960), Machado with Jiménez (1974), Neruda (1975), Vallejo (1976), and Paz (1979).
5. See *Las Cenizas de la Huella: linajes y figuras de artista en torno al modernismo*, ed. by Susana Zanetti (Rosario: Viterbo Editora, 1997), 139. See also Vallejo's homage to Darío in "Retablo" included in *Los Heraldos Negros* (Madrid: Cátedra, 1998).
6. Pablo Neruda, *Confieso que he vivido. Memorias* (Barcelona: Seix Barral, 1974), 161. See also Neruda's homage to Darío in "R.D." included in *Barcarola* (Buenos Aires: Losada, 1967).
7. *Estudios sobre Rubén Darío*, ed. by Ernesto Mejía Sánchez (Mexico: Fondo de Cultura Económica, 1968), 13. Borges borrows the idea of calling Darío "El Libertador" from Leopoldo Lugones's obituary for the Nicaraguan writer, in which the latter elaborates the idea at length by comparing Darío's legacy with that of historical figures such as Simón Bolívar and Domingo Sarmiento. See Leopoldo Lugones, *Rubén Darío* (Buenos Aires: Ediciones Selectas América, 1916).
8. Tomás Navarro Tomás, *Métrica española: reseña histórica y descriptiva* (New York: Las Américas, 1966), 201.
9. See Keith Ellis's assertion from 1974: "Literary criticism on Rubén Darío's work first appeared in 1884 when he was seventeen years old. Since that time the volume of writings devoted to his work has probably become greater than that dealing with any other figure in the history of Spanish American literature" in

Keith Ellis, *Critical Approaches to Rubén Darío* (Toronto: Toronto University Press, 1974), ix.

See also Woodbridge's remark from 1975: "I feel that the work and the critical studies of Darío are so numerous that a group of scholars ought to work on a bibliography of the poet" in Charles Hensley Woodbridge, *Rubén Darío, a Selective Classified and Annotated Bibliography* (Metuchen, NJ: Scarecrow, 1975), 201.

10 Rubén Darío, *Songs of Life and Hope*, trans. by Will Derusha and Alberto Acereda (North Carolina: Duke University Press, 2004), 12.

11 For more comprehensive, if somewhat outdated, surveys and bibliographies, see: Arnold Armand del Greco, *Repertorio bibliográfico del mundo de Rubén Darío* (New York: Las Américas, 1969); José Jirón Terán, *Bibliografía general de Rubén Darío (julio 1883–enero 1967)* (Managua: Comisión Nacional del Centenario, 1967); in addition to Ellis and Woodbridge.

12 For example see Evelyn Picón Garfield and Iván A. Schulman, *"Las entrañas del vacío": ensayos sobre la modernidad hispanoamericana* (Mexico: Ediciones Cuadernos Americanos, 1984); Alejandro Mejías-López, *The Inverted Conquest: The Myth of Modernity and the Transatlantic Onset of Modernism* (Nashville: Vanderbilt University Press, 2009); Mariano Siskind, *Cosmopolitan Desires: Global Modernity and World Literature in Latin America* (Evanston: Northwestern University Press, 2014); among others.

13 Darío had many detractors during his lifetime (one of the most notable being Leopoldo Alas "Clarín"). Later detractors include Mario Benedetti and Enrique Lihn, who, at the height of the Cuban Revolution, read Darío's work as escapist and Europeanized (See Ellis, 36). Luis Cernuda heavily criticized Darío's work, too, though he showed scant knowledge of it. For details of this controversy see Cccil M. Bowra, *Rubén Darío en Oxford* (Managua: Academia nicaragüense de la lengua, 1966). For the ambivalent relation of other Spanish American writers to Darío, such as José Emilio Pacheco and Juan José Saer, see Gwen Kirkpatrick, "Forgiving Rubén Darío," *Review: Literature and Arts of the Americas*, vol. 51, no. 2 (2018), 180–7.

14 Rubén Darío, *Obras completas*, 5 vols (Madrid: A. Aguado, 1950-55), II, 19.

15 The Nicaraguan scholar Leonel Delgado has discussed how Darío's framing of his autobiography sets the tone to which his life story was to be read. See Leonel Delgado, "La vida de Rubén Darío escrita por él mismo. Escritura autobiográfica y políticas del nombre," *Istmo*, vol. 10 (enero–junio 2005), http://istmo.denison.edu/n10/articulos/vida.html#end3 [accessed June 2, 2019].

16 I have been critical of biographies of Darío in Carlos F. Grigsby, "El fracaso de París: Rubén Darío's Modernista Campaign in France," *MLR*, vol. 114, no. 4 (October 2019), 614–33.

17 It would take a few decades after Darío's death for this view to lose sway. For instance, Max Henríquez Ureña's history of the movement, which gives José Martí his due place in its development, was not published until 1954. Likewise, Iván Schulman's study of the importance of the *modernistas* who preceded Darío (namely José Martí, Manuel Gutiérrez Nájera, José Asunción Silva, and Julián del Casal) was not published until 1966. In this regard, it is no coincidence that Paz makes no mention of Martí in his essay on Darío.

18 José Enrique Rodó, *José Enrique Rodó: crítico literario*, ed. by Jorge Rufinelli (Alicante: Instituto de Cultura Juan Gil-Albert, 1995), 49.

19 The monograph was partially published as a reaction to Mapes's work mentioned earlier, which in Rioseco's opinion exaggerated the French origin of Darío's sources.

20 For more on the findings of the *archivo*, see Luis Sáinz de Medrano, "El Seminario-Archivo «Rubén Darío» de la Universidad Complutense de Madrid," *Anales de Literatura Hispanoamericana*, vol. 32 (2003), 99–102.

21 It can also be found alongside other works in Raimundo Lida, *Rubén Darío, modernismo* (Caracas: Monte Ávila, 1984).

22 To cite an example of relevance, Paz inspired studies on the influence of esoteric beliefs in Darío's poetry, which I explore in the Coda.

23 For more on the topic see Leonard Forster, *The Poet's Tongues: Multilingualism in Literature* (Cambridge: Cambridge University Press, 2009). Also, for an up-to-date overview of the studies into literary multilingualism since, see Albert Rossich, "An Overview of Literary Multilingualism," *Comparative Critical Studies*, vol. 15, no. 1 (2018), 47–67.

24 During the nineteenth century, to write in French alongside one's own language was a common ambition. Notable *fin-de-siècle* writers who cultivated French as a literary language include Jean Moréas from Greece, the US writers Stuart Merrill and Francis Viélé-Griffin, the Cuban poet Augusto de Armas, the German poet Stefan George, the Italian novelist Gabriele D'Annunzio, among others (and, of course, Darío).

25 Claudio Guillén, *Entre lo uno y lo diverso* (Barcelona: Crítica, 1985), 327.

26 See Wilhelm T. Elwert, "L'emploi de langues étrangères comme procédé stylistique," *Revue de littérature comparée*, vol. XXXIV, no. 3 (1960), 409–37; and

Paul Zumthor, "Un problème d'esthétique médiévale: l'utilisation poétique du bilinguisme," *Le Moyen Age*, vol. XV (1960), 301–36; 561–94.

27 See Steven Kellman, *The Translingual Imagination* (Lincoln: University of Nebraska Press, 2000); Michael Cronin, *Translation and Globalization* (London: Routledge, 2003); Juliette Taylor-Batt, *Multilingualism in Modernist Fiction* (London: Palgrave MacMillan, 2013); Yasemin Yildiz, *Beyond the Mother Tongue: The Postmonolingual Condition* (New York: Fordham University Press, 2012). For the study of another major author's overlooked multilingualism, see Michelle Woods, *Kafka Translated* (New York: Bloomsbury, 2013).

28 Some recent monographs that use translation as their focus include Rebecca L. Walkowitz, *Born Translated: The Contemporary Novel in an Age of World Literature* (New York: Columbia University Press, 2015); Ignacio Infante, *After Translation: The Transfer and Circulation of Modern Poetics across the Atlantic* (New York: Fordham University Press, 2013); Emily Apter, *The Translation Zone: A New Comparative Literature* (New Jersey: Princeton University Press, 2006).

29 By contrast, *translatio* morphed into Spanish as *trasladar*.

30 For one example among many of this wider use of the term, see James Clifford's influential anthropological application of the term in James Clifford, *Routes: Travel and Translation in the Late Twentieth Century* (Cambridge, MA: Harvard University Press, 1997). For a more influential work in literary studies with a similar metaphorical application of the term, see Homi K. Bhabha, *The Location of Culture* (London: Routledge, 2004).

31 For other works with this focus, see María Roof, "Rubén Darío en inglés: la poesía," *Revista Casa de las Américas*, no. 282 (enero–marzo/2016), 10–33; Roberto González Echevarría, "The Master of Modernismo," *The Nation*, January 25, 2006, https://www.thenation.com/article/master-modernismo/ [accessed May 10, 2019]; Isabel Díaz, "Traducciones de la obra de Rubén Darío a la lengua inglesa," *Miradas críticas sobre Rubén Darío*, ed. by Nicasio Urbina (Managua: PAVSA, 2005), 281–92; all of which point out the poor quality of existing translations.

32 Rubén Darío, *Escritos inéditos de Rubén Darío*, ed. by Erwin K. Mapes (New York: Instituto de las Españas, 1938), 121.

33 It is worth noting that beyond Borges's characteristic statements along these lines, this understanding of originality is essentially a classicist one.

34 For an account of the role translation played for Anglo-American Modernism, see Steven G. Yao's *Translation and the Languages of Modernismo. Gender, Politics, and Language* (New York: Palgrave, 2003).

35 Kathleen Therese O'Conor-Bater recently published a book-length edition of her translations of Darío, which has not been included in this study for reasons of accessibility and circulation. See Kathleen Therese O'Conor-Bater, *A Bilingual Anthology of Poems by Rubén Darío (1867-1916)* (New York: Edwin Mellen Press, 2015).

Chapter 1

1 Rubén Darío, *A. de Gilbert: biografía de Pedro Balmaceda*, in *Obras completas*, II, 163.
2 Rubén Darío, *Autobiografía* (Buenos Aires: Editorial Universitaria, 1968), 98.
3 *Escritos inéditos de Rubén Darío*, Mapes, 121.
4 Siskind, 214. The poem has been discussed by Francisco Contreras and Saavedora Molina; however, it indeed has not received much attention otherwise.
5 Rubén Darío, *Poesía*, ed. by Ernesto Mejía Sánchez (Caracas: Biblioteca Ayacucho, 1977), 419.
6 Siskind, 214.
7 Cf. these lines from "Canto de esperanza" in *Cantos de vida y esperanza*:
   Verdugos de ideales afligieron la tierra,
     en un pozo de sombra la humanidad se encierra
     con los rudos molosos del odio y la guerra. (ll. 10-2)
8 Siskind, 216.
9 Francisco Contreras, *Rubén Darío: su vida y su obra* (Barcelona: Agencia mundial de librería, 1930), 238.
10 See Saavedra Molina, 135. In "France-Amérique" Darío appears to have rehashed some of the tropes of the controversial poem "Salutación al Águila" included in *El canto errante*. Compare the following lines:
   Águila, existe el Cóndor. Es tu hermano en las grandes alturas.
   Los Andes le conocen y saben que, como tú, mira al Sol.
   May this grand Union have no end, dice el poeta.
   Pueden ambos juntarse, en plenitud de concordia y esfuerzo. (ll. 38-41)

   Que l'aigle plane sur notre immense Amérique
   Et que le condor soit son frère dans l'azur. (ll. 27-8)

11 *Escritos inéditos de Rubén Darío*, Mapes, 121.
12 Jorge Eduardo Arellano, *Azul … de Rubén Darío: Nuevas Perspectivas* (Washington, DC: OEA, 1993), 106.
13 Rubén Darío, *Azul …* (Buenos Aires: La Nación, 1905), 111.
14 *Poesía*, 263.
15 Rubén Darío, *Quince prólogos de Rubén Darío* (Managua: Instituto nicaragüense de cultura, 1967), 25.
16 Ernesto Mejía Sánchez, *Cuestiones rubendarianas* (Madrid: Ediciones de la Revista de Occidente, 1970), 222.
17 Rubén Darío, "Historia de mis libros" in *Obras completas*, I, 196.
18 Arellano, 103.
19 Tomás, 408–10.
20 Darío also published what became the first translation of Mallarmé into Spanish in his rendering of "Les Fleurs" as "Las flores," a literalist translation of the Frenchman's piece. See Alfonso García Morales, "Un artículo desconocido de Rubén Darío: «Mallarmé. Notas para un ensayo futuro»," *Anales de literatura hispanoamericana*, vol. 35 (2006), 31–54. Moreover, he putatively published a translation of the Russian writer Maxim Gorky's novel *Tomás Gordeieff* (1902). The quality of this rendering—in turn a translation of the French version—is as poor as to doubt whether Darío was the actual translator. For more on the topic see George Schanzer-Boris Gaidasz, "Rubén Darío, Traductor de Gorki," *Revista Iberoamericana*, vol. 33, no. 64 (1967), 315–31. All of this notwithstanding, Darío's more imaginative use of translation took place in his own writing.
21 Diego Manuel Sequeira, *Rubén Darío, criollo; o, raíz y médula de su creación poética* (Buenos Aires: Guillermo Kraft Ltda., 1945), 65–6.
22 José Martí, *Obras Completas: Edición Crítica, vol. 13, 1881–1882* (Habana: Centro de estudios martianos, 2010), 90.
23 "Historia de mis libros," 196.
24 Rafael María Baralt, *Diccionario de galicismos, ó sea de las voces, locuciones y frases de la lengua francesca que se han introducido en el habla castellana moderna* (Madrid: Imprenta Nacional, 1853), x.
25 Siskind, 199.
26 For two recent analyses of *Los raros*, see José María Martínez, "Los raros: arquitectura(s), jerarquías y filiaciones," *Zama*, Extraordinario: Homenaje a Rubén Darío (2016), 69–91; and Carlos F. Grigsby, "The Different Lives of Rubén Darío's Los raros," *Bulletin of Spanish Studies*, vol. 95, no. 6 (2018), 679–706.

27 For an overview written by Darío on the international outlook of *Symbolisme*, see Rubén Darío, "Al Dr. Max Nordau," *Crónicas desconocidas 1901–1906*, ed. by Günter Schmigalle (Berlin: Edition Tranvía, 2006), 241–53.
28 Julio Ortega, *Rubén Darío* (Barcelona: Omega, 2003), 167.
29 Derek Attridge, *The Singularity of Literature* (London: Routledge, 2004), 92.
30 I am thinking here of *imitatio* as it was understood by, for example, Horace and Seneca, later theorized by Quintilian and Dionysius of Halicarnassus. Like Darío, pre-modern poets imitated creatively and translingually; however, what makes Darío's multilingualism special is his attempt to position himself within French literary tradition despite writing in Spanish. For an in-depth treatment of *imitatio* see David West and Anthony J. Woodman, eds., *Creative Imitation and Latin Literature* (Cambridge: Cambridge University Press, 1979); and Gian Biagio Conte and Charles Segal, *The Rhetoric of Imitation: Genre and Poetic Memory in Virgil and Other Latin Poets* (Ithaca: Cornell University Press, 1986).
31 Craig Morgan Teicher, *We Begin in Gladness: How Poets Progress* (Minneapolis: Graywolf Press, 2018), 4.
32 Ibid., 91–2.
33 *Autobiografía*, 96.
34 Silviano Santiago, *The Space In-between: Essays on Latin American Culture* (Durham: Duke University Press, 2001), 34.
35 Unlike the Spanish of *Prosas*, in which the lexicon is ridden with Gallicisms, the Gallicisms of *Azul* … are mostly syntactic and, as it were, stylistic. For a detailed discussion of the latter, see Mapes, 39–58, and Juan López-Morillas, "El 'Azul' de Rubén Darío: ¿Galicismo mental o lingüístico?," *Revista Hispánica Moderna*, Año 10, no. 1/2 (January–April 1944), 9–14.
36 "Historia de mis libros," 208.
37 Erwin K. Mapes, *L'influence française dans l'œuvre de Rubén Darío* (Paris: H. Champion, 1925), 70.
38 Ibid., 70–1.
39 Arturo Marasso, *Rubén Darío y su creación poética* (Buenos Aires: Editorial Kapelusz, 1954), 59.
40 Max Henríquez Ureña cites a poem written by Guido Spano for Darío upon his arrival to Buenos Aires in 1893. See Max Henríquez Ureña, *Breve historia del modernismo* (Mexico: Fondo de Cultura Económica, 1954), 49.
41 Alberto Julián Pérez, *La poética de Rubén Darío: crisis post-romántica y modelos literarios modernistas* (Madrid: Orígenes, 1992), 156–7.

42 In "Sinfonía en gris mayor," another poem which alludes to Gautier's poem in an even more overt manner (and for that reason has not gone unnoticed by critics), Darío does seem to take up the French poet's exploration of color: He develops several metaphors related to the color gray in a poem that reads as a postcard from the tropics. The result, however, is an altogether different poem about ennui, the melancholy of travel, and homesickness.

43 Iris Zavala, "Sobre la elaboración de 'Cosas del Cid' de Rubén Darío," *Hispanic Review*, vol. 47, no. 2 (1979), 125–47 (127–8).

44 Rubén Darío, *Los raros*, ed. by Günter Schmigalle (Berlin: Verlag Walter Frey, 2015), 400.

45 See Eugénio de Castro, *Obras poéticas*, 10 vols (Lisboa: Imprensa Nacional, 1923), III.

46 "El renacimiento latino" is the term Darío uses in *Los raros* to refer to international *Symbolisme* in so-called "Latin" countries, namely Portugal, Italy, France, and those of Latin America. Note that, tellingly, previous to the influence of *Modernismo* in the Peninsula, Spain was not included in the list. See *Los raros*, 380.

47 For an analysis of how *Prosas profanas* and *Los raros* relate, see Grigsby 2018.

48 "Al acabar de leer la obra de Fra Domenico Cavalca siéntese la impresión de una blanda brisa llena de aromas paradisíacos y refrescantes. Hay algo de infantil que deleita y pone en los labios a veces una suave sonrisa" (*Los raros*, 251).

49 Francisco López Estrada, *Rubén Darío y la edad media: una perspectiva poco conocida sobre la vida y obra del escritor* (Barcelona: Planeta, 1971), 91.

50 "Historia de mis libros," 212.

51 See Alfonso García Morales, "Paralela/mente 'El reino interior' como la 'obra maestra' de Rubén Darío," *Anales de Literatura Española*, no. 28 (2016), 99–117.

52 *Los raros*, 237.

53 Marasso, 140.

54 Chasca analyzes both poems comparatively. See Edmundo Chasca, "El 'Reino interior' de Rubén Darío y 'Crimen amoris' de Verlaine," *Revista Iberoamericana*, vol. 21 (1965), 309–17.

55 *Parallèlement* (1889) is the name of a collection of poems published by Verlaine.

56 Marasso, 140.

57 Santiago, 31–2.

58 The single line in all Darío's oeuvre that epitomizes this characteristic is "Con Hugo fuerte y con Verlaine ambiguo" from the opening poem of *Cantos de vida y esperanza*. As a poet, Darío unabashedly defined himself according to his influences.

59 Gerard Aching, "The Temporalities of Modernity in Spanish American Modernismo: Darío's Bourgeois King," *The Oxford Handbook of Global Modernisms*, ed. by Mark Wollaeger and Matt Eatough (Oxford: Oxford University Press, 2012), 109-29 (115).
60 *A. de Gilbert*, 161.
61 One could even think here of *aemulatio*, in addition to *imitatio*, in the classical sense of the word. That is, of allusions to other authors that are emulative insofar as they wish to match or surpass the model with whom they compete. For a discussion of *aemulatio*, see Gian Biagio Conte and Charles Segal, 26-66.

Chapter 2

1 Zavala, 127.
2 In particular, see Mapes, Paz, and Salinas, quoted *sic passim* in this book.
3 The evolution and main consequences of this cultural movement have been analyzed in detail by Litvak. See Lily Litvak, *España 1900: modernismo, anarquismo y fin de siglo* (Barcelona: Antropos, 1990), 155-92.
4 Escritos inéditos de Rubén Darío, Mapes, 162.
5 Some decades earlier, in his ground-breaking *Gramática de la lengua castellana destinada al uso de los americanos* (1847), Andrés Bello had proposed orthographical changes for Spanish American users of the language.
6 It is worth noting that, while critics have for the most part accepted Nieva's *Cancionero* as Darío's source (José María de Cossío would build on that discovery to analyze the meter of the poems in relation to their source), Andrés Quintián cites Darío's articles "Una nueva traducción del Dante" and "El castellano de Víctor Hugo" as proof of the Nicaraguan's early familiarity with the history of fifteenth-century Spanish poetry and with anthologies that included some of the Provençal poets rewritten in "Dezires." In other words, he points to alternative or complementary sources for the poems which should be taken into account. See Andrés R. Quintián, *Cultura y literatura españolas en Rubén Darío* (Madrid: Gredos, 1974), 138-42.
7 Pedro Henríquez Ureña, "Rubén Darío y el siglo XV," *Revue Hispanique*, vol. L (1920), 324-7 (324-5).
8 Quintián, 135.
9 Ureña, 325.
10 The "copla esparza" was a genre of Provençal poetry cultivated by Castilian, Catalan, and Aragonese poets. Around eight lines long, they were traditionally

brief and light-hearted compositions on the theme of love. For more information, see Miguel Ángel Perez Priego, "'Dezires, layes y canciones' de Prosas profanas," *Anales de Literatura Española*, no. 28 (2016), 171–97 (171–84).

11 Marasso, 230–4.
12 Miguel de Cervantes, *Don Quijote de la Mancha* (Barcelona: Galaxia Gutenberg, 2004), 650–51.
13 It should be said that Darío's reappraisal of Góngora predates that of the *Generación del 27*, encouraged perhaps by the fact that both Moréas and Verlaine had shown interest in the Spanish poet.
14 See Luis de Góngora y Argote, *Romance de Angélica y Medoro: estudio-comentario*, ed. by Dámaso Alonso (Madrid: Ediciones Acies, 1962).
15 Octavio Paz, *Cuadrivio: Darío, López Velarde, Pessoa, Cernuda* (Mexico: Joaquín Mortiz, 1965), 45.
16 "Historia de mis libros," 215.
17 Priego, 171–97.
18 Sylvia Molloy, "Voracidad y solipsismo en la poesía de Darío," *Zama*, Extraordinario: Rubén Darío (2016), 311–17 (311).
19 *Crónicas desconocidas*, I, 45–6.
20 For further details, see Marasso 91. For an overview of Darío's first classical readings see "Las humanidades de Rubén Darío" in *Cuestiones rubendarianas*, 141–59. For a general survey of Greco-Roman tropes in Darío's oeuvre, see Dolores Ackel Fiore, *Rubén Darío in Search of Inspiration: Greco-Roman Mythology in His Stories and Poetry* (New York: Las Américas, 1963).
21 Other poems such as "Un soneto a Cervantes" are also texts about reading:
Horas de pesadumbre y de tristeza,
paso en mi soledad. Pero Cervantes
es buen amigo. Endulza mis instantes. (ll. 1–3)
22 See José Agustín Balseiro, *Seis estudios sobre Rubén Darío* (Madrid: Gredos, 1967), 103–17.
23 Osvaldo Bazil, "Biografía de Rubén Darío," *Rubén Darío y sus amigos dominicanos*, ed. by Emilio Rodríguez Demorizi (Bogotá: Ediciones Espiral, 1948), 131–227 (141–57).
24 For more information on Darío's struggles with French, see Grigsby 2019.
25 *Poesía*, 243.
26 "Historia de mis libros," 216.
27 Julio Saavedra Molina, *Los hexámetros castellanos y en particular los de Rubén Darío* (Santiago: Prensas de la Universidad de Chile, 1935), 67.

28 Molina, 37.
29 Ibid., 62.
30 Ibid., 72.
31 Marasso, 186–7.
32 Ibid., 187.
33 The poem created widespread controversy for advocating a union between the United States and Latin America, in direct contradiction with Darío's earlier and famous anti-imperialist poem "A Roosevelt" from *Cantos de vida y esperanza*.
34 Saavedra omits "«In memoriam» Bartolomé Mitre" in his study of Darío's hexameters.
35 Et toi, Paris! magicienne de la Race,
   reine latine, éclaire notre jour obscur.
   Donnez-nous le secret que votre pas nous trace,
   et la force du *Fluctuat nec mergitur* ! (ll. 29–33)
36 The poems "Visión" and "Revelación," from *El canto errante*, are both written in Dante's *terza rima*.
37 Both were published serially in *La Nación*.
38 See Grigsby 2019, footnote 59 (736).
39 See Virgil, *Eclogues. Georgics. Aeneid: Books* 1–6, trans. by H. Rushton Fairclough. Revised by G. P. Goold. Loeb Classical Library 63 (Cambridge, MA: Harvard University Press, 1916), 66–7.
40 Some critics have taken this only as an allusion, and a response, to an earlier poem written by Lugones for Darío called "A Rubén Darío," which was published in the newspaper *Athenas* in Córdoba, Argentina, in 1903. See Carmen Ruiz Barrionuevo. *Rubén Darío*. Madrid, 2002 [134]; and Susana Zannetti, "Rubén Darío, cosmopolitismo y errancia: «Epístola a la señora de Leopoldo Lugones»," *Actas del III Congreso Internacional CELEHIS de Literatura (Española, Latinoamericana y Argentina)*, no. 19 (2008), 131–58. In contrast to them, I argue that Darío is dialoguing here with Lugones in a wider sense—and with other young *modernistas* of the time, such as Manuel Machado and Julio Herrera y Reissig—as can be seen in the similarities of style in other poems of *El canto errante* such as "Agencia," "Dream," "Tan mieux …, " and "«Eheu»". Considering the years of publication, this also seems the more likely hypothesis.
41 Rubén Darío, *Obras Completas I* (Barcelona: Galaxia Gutenberg, 2007), 949–59.

Chapter 3

1. Lawrence Venuti, *The Translator's Invisibility: A History of Translation* (London: Routledge, 2008), 228.
2. Esther Allen and Susan Bernofsky (eds.), *In Translation: Translators on Their Work and What It Means* (New York: Columbia University Press, 2013), 83–93.
3. Peter Hulme, *The Dinner at Gonfarone's: Salomón de La Selva and his pan-American Project in Nueva York, 1915–1919* (Liverpool: Liverpool University Press, 2019), 139.
4. Sturgis E. Leavitt, "The Teaching of Spanish in the United States," *Hispania*, vol. 44, no. 4 (December 1961), 591–625 (612).
5. Jeremy Munday, *Style and Ideology in Translation: Latin American Writing in English* (London: Routledge, 2007), 51–4.
6. Deborah Cohn, "A Tale of Two Translation Programs: Politics, the Market, and Rockefeller Funding for Latin American Literature in the United States during the 1960s and 1970s," *Latin American Research Review*, vol. 41, no. 2 (2006), 139–64 (154).
7. See Irene Rostagno, *Searching for Recognition: The Promotion of Latin American Literature in the United States* (Westport: Greenwood Press, 1997).
8. Cecil M. Bowra, *Inspiration and Poetry* (London: Macmillan, 1955), 244–5.
9. The dates are similar also in the cases of other important Latin American centers, such as those of the Universities of Liverpool and Glasgow. See Craskke and Lehmann.
10. Nikki Craskke and David Lehmann, "Fifty Years of Research in Latin American Studies in the UK," *Revista europea de estudios latinoamericanos y del caribe/European Review of Latin American and Caribbean Studies*, no. 72 (2002), 61–80 (61).
11. See *Trilce*, trans. by Valentino Gianuzzi and Michael Smith (Exeter: Shearsman Books, 2005); *Scales: Melographed*, trans. by Joseph Mulligan (Middletown: Wesleyan University Press, 2017); *Spain, Take This Chalice from Me and Other Poems*, trans. by Margaret Sayers Peden (New York: Penguin, 2008); and *The Complete Poetry: A Bilingual Edition*, trans. by Clayton Eshelman and José R. Barcia (Berkely: University of California Press, 2009).
12. See Ian Watts, *The Rise of the Novel: Studies in Defoe, Richardson and Fielding* (London: Pimlico, 2000). For a comparative account of the novel, see Franco Moretti, *Distant Reading* (London: Verso, 2003).

13 See Sturgis E. Leavis, *Hispano-American Literature in the United States: A Bibliography of Translations and Criticism* (Stanford: Stanford University Press, 1932).

14 Hulme, 44.

15 J. Fred Rippy, "Literary Yankeephobia in Hispanic America," *The Journal of International Relations*, vol. 12, no. 3 (January 1922), 350.

16 Albert Mordell, "Sketch of Hon. Charles B. McMichael," *Reminiscences and Essays*, ed. by Charles B. McMichael (Privately printed, 1922), 7–17. I will comment on Darío's sojourn in New York City in the coming pages.

17 Rodó's *Ariel* is itself much more nuanced than *arielismo* as a discourse turned out to be, extolling several virtues of US culture before criticizing it for its spiritual and artistic hollowness.

18 Williams also published a translation of Guatemalan writer Rafael Martínez Arévalo's "El hombre que parecía un caballo" in December 1918 in *The Little Review*—the magazine where, incidentally, the first installment of James Joyce's *Ulysses* was published. As a translator, Williams worked with the help of his father, who was fluent in Spanish (his mother, Raquel Elena Hoheb Williams, was Puerto Rican). For more on his Hispanic heritage, see Julio Marzán, *The Spanish American Roots of William Carlos Williams* (Austin: University of Texas Press, 1994). For his translations from the Spanish, which include poems by Nicanor Parra, Octavio Paz, and Eunice Odio, see *By Word of Mouth: Poem from the Spanish, 1916–1959* (New York: New Directions, 2011).

19 Hulme, 225.

20 See *Pan-American Magazine*, September, 1918, 215–78 (https://babel.hathitrust.org/cgi/pt?id=nyp.33433088799170&view=1up&seq=223&q1=*). Regarding information on Blackwell and these early publications, I am indebted to Roofs research done on the topic.

21 See Roof, 12.

22 Hulme, 233.

23 For more on the findings, see Johan Alba Cutler, "Latinx Modernism and the Spirit of Latinoamericanismo," *American Literary History*, vol. 33, no. 3 (Fall 2021), 571–87.

24 Hulme, 91.

25 Ibid., 94–8.

26 "Noted South American Poet Writes about New York," *The New York Times*, November 29, 1916, 98, https://timesmachine.nytimes.com/

timesmachine/1914/11/29/100118658.html?pageNumber=98 [accessed on March 15, 2023].

27 Gerardo Piña-Rosales et al. (eds.), *Rubén Darío y los Estados Unidos* (New York: Academia Norteamericana de la Lengua Española, 2017), 236.
28 As Hulme asserts, ten of these translations were done by de la Selva, and only "Pórtico" had been done by Walsh, even if his name appeared first on the cover. See 138.
29 Muna Lee, "A Painful Example," *Poetry*, vol. 22, no. 3 (June, 1923), 165–8.
30 See Soledad Marambio, *Sujetos del deseo: una exploración sobre la traducción amateur en los años del Panamericanismo* (Berlin/Boston: De Gruyter, 2021) and Harris Feinsod, *The Poetry of the Americas* (Oxford: Oxford University Press, 2017).
31 Thomas Walsh, *Hispanic Anthology* (New York: G.P. Putnam's Sons, 1920), 603.
32 Alice Blackwell (trans.), *Some Spanish American Poets* (New York: Appleton and Company, 1928), XV.
33 Ibid., 182.
34 Ibid., VII–VIII.
35 G. Dundas Craig, *The Modernist Trend in Spanish-American Poetry* (Berkeley: The University of California Press, 1934), 16.
36 Ibid., ix.
37 Ibid., 39.
38 Percy Alvin Martin, "Review of *The Modernist Trend in Spanish American Poetry*," *The Hispanic American Historical Review*, vol. 14, no. 3 (August 1934), 339–40.
39 See Marambio, 115. According to Feinsod, Neruda and Carrera Andrade were the best-known Latin American poets during those decades, with the latter having garnered praise from Wallace Stevens, Carl Sandburg, and William Carlos Williams. See Feinsod, 39.
40 Ibid., 28.
41 See Hulme, 33.
42 Dudley Fitts, *Anthology of Contemporary Latin-American Poetry* (New York: New Directions, 1942), xi.
43 See Feinsod, 35.
44 Hays explains in an interview how he was hired by Fitts to do all the biographies of the latter's anthology, which shows how small the translation circles for Spanish-language poetry were at the time. See Johnathan Cohen, "Discovering Neruda: An Interview with H. R. Hays," *Translation Review*, vol. 6 (1980), 32.

45 Ibid., 30.
46 See Hoffman R. Hays, *12 Spanish American Poets* (New Haven: Yale University Press, 1943), 1–21.
47 See Cohen, 32.
48 See Susanne Klengel, "Gabriela Mistral (1945)," *Nobelpreisträgerinnen: 14 Shriftstellerinnen im Porträt*, ed. by Claudia Olk and Susanne Zepp (Berlin: De Gruyter, 2019), 96.
49 See Elizabeth Horen, "Unrepentant Traveler, Accidental Diplomat, Triumphant Nobel: Gabriela Mistral in Wartime Brazil," *Anales de Literatura Chilena*, Año 16, diciembre, 2015, número 24, 253–78 (262). Horen reconstructs the lead-up to Mistral's Nobel prize, perceptively discerning the politics behind it and laying out Mistral's own active and vested role in her Nobel campaign.
50 See Marambio, 115.
51 For more details, see Marambio, 117–8.
52 Langston Hughes, *Selected poems of Gabriela Mistral* (London: Indiana University Press, 1972), 10.
53 Venuti, 164.
54 André Lefevere, *Translation, Rewriting, and the Manipulation of Literary Fame* (London: Routledge, 1992), 99–100.
55 Venuti, 178.
56 The belatedness was already acknowledged by Arthur Symons in a note to the first edition of *The Symbolist Movement in Literature* (1899), which largely introduced the movement to Anglophone readers, where he discusses *Symbolisme*'s international influence at the time:

> In Germany it seems to be permeating the whole of literature, its spirit is that which is deepest in Ibsen, it has absorbed the one new force in Italy, Gabriele d'Annunzio. I am told of a group of Symbolists in Russian Literature, there is another in Dutch literature, in Portugal it has a little school of its own under Eugenio de Castro; I even saw some faint strivings that way in Spain, and the aged Spanish poet Campoamor has always fought on behalf of a "transcendental" art in which we should recognise much of what is most essential in the doctrine of Symbolism.

See Arthur Symons, *The Symbolist Movement in Literature*, ed. by Matthew Creasy (Manchester: Carcanet, 2014), 3. Three years earlier, Darío had published *Los raros* and *Prosas profanas* in Argentina.

57 Peter Childs, *Modernism* (London: Routledge, 2017), 99–101.
58 To underline the commonalities, it is worth noting that Darío and Pound were both greatly influenced by Rémy de Gourmont and Théophile Gautier, besides their common interest in troubadour poetry. Another salient point of contact between *modernistas* and modernists concerns the influence of Jules Laforgue, who was a key reading for T. S. Eliot and Leopoldo Lugones.
59 Octavio Paz, *Los hijos del limo* (Barcelona: Seix Barral, 1974), 126.
60 Mejías-López, 21.
61 For an overview of its large impact upon these writers, see Matthew Creasy's introduction to *The Symbolist Movement*, x–xxix.
62 Symons, xiii.
63 "After we have read Verlaine and Laforgue and Rimbaud and return to Mr. Symons' book, we may find that our own impressions dissent from his. The book has not, perhaps, a permanent value for the one reader, but it has led to results of permanent importance for him." See Thomas S. Eliot, *The Sacred Wood: Essays on Poetry and Criticism* (London: Methuen, 1970), 5.
64 Symons, 177. Nor does Moréas appear in recent revaluations of the *fin de siècle*, such as in Vincent Sherry's otherwise excellent *Modernism and the Reinvention of Decadence* (Cambridge: Cambridge University Press, 2015).
65 Ibid., 7.
66 See David Weir, *Decadence and the Making of Modernism* (Amherst: University of Massachusetts Press, 1995).
67 Murray Pittock, *Spectrum of Decadence: The Literature of the 1890s* (London: Routledge, 1993), 71.
68 Pittock, 77.
69 Frank Kermode's discussion of Symon's influence is also relevant: "That *The Symbolist Movement* is absolutely a good book I suppose nobody would suggest. It is scrappy, lacking the pertinacity we have come to expect from critics; it is often disagreeably imprecise. As a simple exposition of its subject it has of course been superseded. But it is a very good place to look if one wants to know how French Symbolism struck a well-informed, avant-garde Paterian in the nineties; and considering that the character of modern poetry has been, to a remarkable degree, formed by that contact, we may well think it worthwhile to do so." See Frank Kermode, *Romantic Image* (London: Routledge, 2002), 127–40 (128–9).
70 Symons, xx.
71 Sherry, 9.

72　This is not to discredit the importance of the *vers libre* he did write, such as in "Heraldos" from *Prosas profanas*. Despite mostly writing in rhyme, Darío was one of the introducers of *vers libre* in Spanish.

73　For more information on *vers libéré*, see Scott 2012, 310.

74　Cf. Alejandro Mejías-López's critique of the Anglo—and Eurocentric biases present in concepts of literary modernism, which have cast aside *Modernismo* and Latin America from narratives of modernity. Mejías-López, 16–56.

75　Carlos Martínez Rivas, "Watteau y su siglo en Rubén Darío," *Cuadernos Hispanoamericanos*, no. 212 (1967), 445–53 (446).

76　Rubén Darío, *Peregrinaciones* (Paris: Imprenta de la Vda de Ch. Bouret, 1901), 83–4.

77　Ibid., 88–9.

78　Rivers of ink have run on the topic of the influences of *Modernismo*, whether classical, medieval, early modern, or modern. In the case of Darío's classicism specifically, Marasso remains the best source on the matter, as well as Mejía Sánchez and Fiore. However, if we are to look at what Darío himself wrote, besides the evident neo-classicism of *Abrojos* (1887) and the classicism of his works from *Cantos de vida y esperanza* (1905) on, this passage from the preface to *El canto errante*, "Dilucidaciones," is worth citing in full by way of illustration:

> Y mis aficiones clásicas encontraban un consuelo con la amistosa conversación de cierto joven maestro [...] Amador de la lectura clásica, me he nutrido de ella, mas siguiendo el paso de mis días. He comprendido la fuerza de las tradiciones en el pasado, y de las previsiones en lo futuro.

See *Poesía*, 303–5.

79　Ibid., 93.

80　The case of the poet Rainer Maria Rilke, who actively sought to live close to Rodin and went as far as working as his secretary to that end, stands in stark contrast to the Nicaraguan. Rilke considered Rodin the embodiment of modern art. It is instructional to consider that Rilke and Darío lived in Paris at the same time, and were exposed to similar artworks, despite the vast differences between their oeuvres. For more on Rilke's time working for Rodin see Donald Prater, *A Ringing Glass: The Life of Rainer Maria Rilke* (Oxford: Oxford University Press, 1994), 89–133.

81　Rubén Darío, *Letras*, in *Obras completas*, I, 618.

82　Ibid., 209.

83 This would make Darío one of Rimbaud's first commentators in Spanish, considering that his passing references to him in *Los raros* date from as early as 1896. Darío was also one of the first commentators and translators of Lautréamont. For more information on the translations of Rimbaud in Spanish, see José Francisco Ruiz Casanova, "Arthur Rimbaud," *Diccionario histórico de la traducción en España*, ed. by Francisco Lafarga and Luis Pegenaute (Madrid: Gredos, 2009), 974–5. For information on Darío and Lautréamont, see Publio González-Rodas, "Rubén Darío y el Conde de Lautréamont," *Revista Iberoamericana*, vol. 37, no. 75 (1971), 375–89.

84 Rubén Darío, "Un nuevo libro sobre Arthur Rimbaud," *Escritos dispersos de Rubén Darío*, ed. by Pedro Luis Barcia (La Plata: Universidad Nacional de la Plata, 1968), 308–16 (313).

85 Ibid., 314.

86 Ibid., 309.

87 "With Victor Hugo, with Baudelaire, we are still under the dominion of rhetoric. 'Take eloquence, and wring its neck!' said Verlaine in his *Art Poétique*; and he showed, by writing it, that French verse could be written without rhetoric. [...] There are poems of Verlaine which go as far as verse can go to become pure music, the voice of a bird with a human soul." See Symons, 45–6.

88 Beatriz Colombi, "Rubén Darío y Auguste Rodin: modernidades desfasadas," *CELEHIS*, no. 33 (2017), 27–38 (32).

89 Likewise, Rama speaks of *una modernidad discrónica*, while Julio Ramos calls it *una modernidad desencontrada*. See Ángel Rama, *Las mascaras democráticas del modernismo* (Montevideo: Arca, 1985) and Julio Ramos, *Desencuentros de la modernidad en América Latina* (Mexico: Fondo de Cultura Económica, 1989).

90 On the other hand, I am less convinced by Jameson's insistence on the notion that we live in "postmodern" times, as opposed to a late stage of modernity which may or may not be at the doorstep of a new era, as the sociologist Anthony Giddens holds. For a lucid discussion of these two theories in comparison, see Laura Lonsdale, *Multilingualism and Modernity: Barbarisms in Spanish and American Literature* (Cham: Palgrave Macmillan, 2017), 14–15. For a specifically Latin American context, see Rama 1985.

91 Bowra 1966, 97–8.

92 *Los raros*, 78.

93 Steven White, "Salomón de la Selva: Testimonial Poetry and World War I," *Modern Nicaraguan Poetry: Dialogues with France and the United States* (London: Associated University Press, 1993), 119–43 (120).
94 As Hulme reminds us echoing Henríquez Ureña, "de la Selva's poetic heroes were Francis Thompson and John Keats, his critical muses Alice Keynell and Walter Pater" (242).
95 White, 120–1. For more information on de la Selva's influences at the time, see Salomón de la Selva, *Tropical Town and Other Poems*, ed. by Silvio Sirias (Houston: Arte Público Press, 1997), 1–61. According to Sirias, *Tropical Town* is now considered the first English-language collection of poetry written by a Hispanic writer in the United States. It also remains virtually unstudied (1). See White's chapter on the poet for further discussion.
96 José Emilio Pacheco, "Nota sobre la otra Vanguardia," *Revista Iberoamericana*, vol. 45, no. 106 (1979), 327–34 (327–31).
97 Cohen, 179.
98 Rachel J. Galvin, "Poetic Innovation and Appropriative Translation in the Americas," *A Companion to Translation Studies*, ed. by Sandra Bermann and Catherine Porter (Oxford: Wiley Blackwell, 2014), 361–74 (362).
99 See Pablo Neruda, *Twenty Love Poems and a Song of Despair*, trans. by William S. Merwin (New York: Penguin, 2003); Galvin, 361; and Cohen, 182.
100 Robert Bly, *Neruda and Vallejo: Selected Poems* (Boston: Beacon Press, 1962), 69.
101 Deborah Cohn, *The Latin American Literary Boom and U.S. Nationalism during the Cold War* (Nashville: Vanderbilt University Press, 2012), 73.
102 Galvin, 363.
103 Kenneth Koch, *The Collected Poems* (New York: Knopf, 2018), 195.
104 Johnathan Mayhew, *Apocryphal Lorca: Translation, Parody, Kitsch* (Chicago: Chicago University Press, 2009), xii.
105 Its links to Modernism and its role as social practice have been astutely studied by Jeremy Braddock. See Jeremy Braddock, *Collecting as Modernist Practice* (Baltimore: Johns Hopkins University Press, 2013).
106 Scott Douglas Challener, *From the Outside: Latin American Anthologies and the Making of U.S. Literature*. October 2019, Rutgers University, PhD Dissertation, 10.
107 A host of other factors, which are clearly laid out by Cohn in her article, also came into play when considering the different degrees of success of the two translation programs. See 139–64.
108 Cohn, 153.

109 In Feinsod's opinion, Kemp is, besides Rabassa and Onís, "the most prolific and important—if least heralded—US broker of Boom-era Latin American literature." See Feinsod, 88. His translations of Darío are also the most represented in anthologies where the *modernista*'s poetry is included.

110 Just a few years earlier, Samuel Beckett's translations of Mexican Poetry, compiled by Octavio Paz, were also published in 1958 on their own—that is, monolingually.

111 I am not including here two booklets that were published in this interim: Helen Wohl Patterson's *Rubén Darío y Nicaragua. Bilingual Anthology of Poetry* (1966) and Edward Loomis's *El Nica and Don Antonio: Translations from the Spanish of Rubén Darío and Machado* (2000). As Roof explains, these circulated scarcely. It was not possible to access them for this study. See Roof, 16–19.

112 Munday, 98.

113 For more on Bolaño's reception and exoticists expectations at play, see Sarah Pollack, "Latin America Translated (Again): Roberto Bolaño's *The Savage Detectives* in the United States," *Comparative Literature*, vol. 61, no. 3 (2009), 346–65.

114 In his introduction to the translations, he wistfully comments on the possibility of hearing Darío in English as one of his long-held dreams as a Latinx immigrant.

115 José Emilio Pacheco, "Prólogo 'Rubén Darío entre dos siglos,'" *Obras Completas I de Rubén Darío* (Barcelona: Galaxia Gutenberg, 2007), 46.

116 *Songs of Life and Hope*, 1.

117 Ibid., 6.

118 Jorge Luis Borges, *Jorge Luis Borges en Sur (1931–1980)* (Buenos Aires: Emecé, 1999), 321–2.

119 Eliot, 33.

120 Ezra Pound, *Literary Essays of Ezra Pound*, ed. by T. S. Eliot (London: Faber and Faber, 1954), 25.

121 Venuti, 49–50.

122 Stanley Appelbaum, *Stories and Poems/Cuentos y Poesías: A Dual-Language Book* (Mineola, NY: Dover Publications, 2002), xiii.

123 Ibid., xii.

124 *Songs of Life and Hope*, 2.

125 Ibid., 3.

126 Ibid., 6.

127 One can compare it with Ernesto Mejía Sánchez's canonical edition of *Poesía* (1977) for confirmation. It is worth pointing out that, unlike the Nicaraguan scholar, Derusha/Acereda follow Darío's punctuation marks strictly (whose original manuscripts do not show any opening exclamation and interrogation marks), which most editions standardize.

Coda: Translating Darío's Poetics of *(H)armonía*

1. *Poesía*, 180.
2. Ibid., 304.
3. Guillermo Sucre, *La máscara, la transparencia: ensayos sobre poesía hispanoamericana* (Caracas: Monte Ávila, 1975), 41.
4. Catherine Jrade, *Rubén Darío and the Romantic Search for Unity* (Texas: University of Texas Press, 1983), 17.
5. The belief was also shared by many *modernistas*: see Theodore W Jensen, "El pitagorismo en Las fuerzas extrañas de Lugones," *Otros mundos otros fuegos: Fantasía y realismo mágico en Iberoamérica, Memoria del XVI Congreso Internacional de Literatura Iberoamericana*, ed. by Donald A. Yates (East Lansing: Michigan State University, 1975), 299–307; Antonio Risco, *El demiurgo y su mundo: hacia un nuevo enfoque de la obra de Valle-Inclán* (Madrid: Gredos, 1997); Iván Schulman, "Modernismo, revolución y pitagorismo en Martí," *Casa de la Américas*, no. 73 (1972), 45–55.
6. Raymond Skyrme, *Darío and the Pythagorean Tradition* (Gainesville: University Presses of Florida, 1975), 91–2.
7. Sucre, 42.
8. Julián Pérez, 125–8.
9. Jitrik looks at the writing of *Modernismo* as a combinatorial system based on accent and sounds, which managed to spread across Spanish America effectively thanks to its systemic regularities. On the other hand, Lorenz analyzes the wide presence of musical tropes in Darío's oeuvre and explicates the importance of music in his poetics.
10. *Poesía*, 236–7.
11. Jean Boase-Beier, "Translating the Eye of the Poem," *CTIS* Occasional Papers, no. 5 (2009), 1–20 (11–2).
12. Enrique Anderson Imbert, *La originalidad de Rubén Darío* (Buenos Aires: Centro Editor de América Latina, 1967), 81.

Bibliography

Aching, Gerard, "The Temporalities of Modernity in Spanish American Modernismo: Darío's Bourgeois King," *The Oxford Handbook of Global Modernisms*, ed. by Mark Wollaeger and Matt Eatough (Oxford: Oxford University Press, 2012): 109–29.

Aguado-Andreut, Salvador, *Por el mundo poético de Rubén Darío* (Guatemala: Editorial Universitaria, 1966).

Agustini, Delmira, *Los cálices vacíos* (Buenos Aires: Ediciones Simurg, 1999).

Alba Cutler, John, "Latinx Modernism and the Spirit of Latinoamericanismo," *American Literary History*, vol. 33, no. 3 (Fall 2021): 571–87.

Allen, Esther and Susan Bernofsky, eds., *In Translation: Translators on Their Work and What It Means* (New York: Columbia University Press, 2013).

Anderson Imbert, Enrique, *La originalidad de Rubén Darío* (Buenos Aires: Centro Editor de América Latina, 1967).

Appelbaum, Stanley, *Stories and Poems/Cuentos y Poesías: A Dual-Language Book* (Mineola, NY: Dover Publications, 2002).

Apter, Emily S., *The Translation Zone: A New Comparative Literature* (New Jersey: Princeton University Press, 2006).

Arellano, Jorge Eduardo, *Azul ... de Rubén Darío: Nuevas Perspectivas* (Washington, DC: OEA, 1993).

Arévalo Martínez, Rafael, "The Man Who Resembled a Horse," trans. by William Carlos Williams, *The Little Review*, vol. 5, no. 8 (December 1918): 42–53.

Attridge, Derek, *The Singularity of Literature* (London: Routledge, 2004).

Balderston, Daniel, "Celedonio Flores's 'Sonatina': Lunfardo Parody and Post-Modernist Esthetics," *Hispania*, vol. 72, no. 1 (1989): 123–9.

Banville, Théodore de, *Odes Funambulesques: suivies d'un commentaire* (Paris: A. Lemerre, 1873).

Baralt, Rafael María, *Diccionario de galicismos, ó sea de las voces, locuciones y frases de la lengua francesca que se han introducido en el habla castellana moderna* (Madrid: Imprenta Nacional, 1855).

Barcia, Pedro L., *Rubén Darío: entre el Tango y el lunfardo* (Buenos Aires: Consulado del Uruguay, 1997).

Barisone, José Alberto, "El eco de Rubén Darío en letras de tango," *RECIAL: Revista del centro de investigaciones de la facultad de filosofía y humanidades, áreas letras*, vol. 7, no. 10 (2016): 8–33.

Bellos, David, *Is That a Fish in Your Ear?* (London: Penguin, 2012).

Benjamin, Walter, *Illuminations* (New York: Schocken Books, 1986).

Berceo, Gonzalo de, *Vida de Santo Domingo de Silos* (Madrid: Castalia, 1973).

Bhabha, Homi K., *The Location of Culture* (London: Routledge, 2004).

Blackwell, Alice, *Some Spanish American Poets* (New York: Appleton and Company, 1928).

Bly, Robert, *Neruda and Vallejo: Selected Poems* (Boston: Beacon Press, 1962).

Boase-Beier, Jean, *A Critical Introduction to Translation Studies* (London: Continuum, 2011).

Boase-Beier, Jean, "Stylistics and Translation," *The Oxford Handbook of Translation Studies*, ed. by Kirsten Malmkjær and Kevin Windle (Oxford: Oxford University Press, 2011): 71–83.

Boase-Beier, Jean, "Translating the Eye of the Poem," *CTIS Occasional Papers*, no. 5 (2009): 1–20.

Boll, Tom, "Penguin Books and the Translation of Spanish and Latin American Poetry, 1956–1979," *Translation & Literature*, vol. 25, no. 1 (2016): 28–57.

Borges, Jorge Luis, *Discusión* (Buenos Aires: Gleizer, 1932).

Borges, Jorge Luis, *Jorge Luis Borges en Sur (1931–1980)* (Buenos Aires: Emecé, 1999).

Bowra, Cecil M., *Inspiration and Poetry* (London: Macmillan, 1955).

Bowra, Cecil M., *Rubén Darío en Oxford* (Managua: Academia nicaragüense de la lengua, 1966).

Braddock, Jeremy, *Collecting as Modernist Practice* (Baltimore: Johns Hopkins University Press, 2013).

Caresani, Rodrigo, "Hieratismo en movimiento: Rubén Darío, Stéphane Mallarmé y 'La página blanca,'" *Revista de Estudios Hispánicos*, vol. 51, no. 1 (2017): 127–47.

Carne-Ross, Donald S., *Classics and Translation: Essays* (Lewisburg, PA: Bucknell University Press, 2010).

Carper, Thomas and Derek Attridge, *Meter and Meaning: An Introduction to Rhythm in Poetry* (London: Routledge, 2003).

Carson, Anne, *Float* (London: Knopf, 2016).

Cervantes, Miguel de, *Don Quijote de la Mancha* (Barcelona: Galaxia Gutenberg, 2004).

Childs, Peter, *Modernism* (London: Routledge, 2017).

Clifford, James, *Routes: Travel and Translation in the Late Twentieth Century* (Cambridge, MA: Harvard University Press, 1997).

Cohen, Johnathan, "Discovering Neruda: An Interview with H.R. Hays," *Translation Review*, vol. 6, (1980): 29–34.

Cohn, Deborah, "A Tale of Two Translation Programs: Politics, the Market, and Rockefeller Funding for Latin American Literature in the United States during the 1960s and 1970s," *Latin American Research Review*, vol. 41, no. 2 (2006): 139–64.

Cohn, Deborah, *The Latin American Literary Boom and U.S. Nationalism during the Cold War* (Nashville: Vanderbilt University Press, 2012).

Colombi, Beatriz, "Rubén Darío y Auguste Rodin: modernidades desfasadas," *CELEHIS*, no. 33 (2017): 27–38.

Conte, Gian Biagio and Charles Segal, *The Rhetoric of Imitation: Genre and Poetic Memory in Virgil and Other Latin Poets* (London: Cornell University Press, 1986).

Contreras, Francisco, *Rubén Darío: su vida y su obra* (Barcelona: Agencia mundial de librería, 1930).

Coppée, François, *Œuvres de François Coppée: Poésies* (Paris: A. Lemerre, 1907).

Cossío, José María de, "El modelo estrófico de los 'Layes, decires y canciones' de Rubén Darío," *Revista de Filología Española*, vol. XIX (1932): 283–7.

Craskke, Niki and David Lehmann, "Fifty Years of Research in Latin American Studies in the UK," *Revista europea de estudios latinoamericanos y del caribe/ European Review of Latin American and Caribbean Studies*, no. 72 (2002): 61–80.

Cronin, Michael, *Translation and Globalization* (London: Routledge, 2003).

Darío, Rubén, *Autobiografía* (Buenos Aires: Editorial Universitaria, 1968).

Darío, Rubén, *Azul* (Buenos Aires: La Nación, 1905).

Darío, Rubén, *Crónicas desconocidas 1901–1906*, ed. by Günther Schmigalle (Berlin: Tranvía, 2006).

Darío, Rubén, *Crónicas desconocidas 1906–1914*, ed. by Günther Schmigalle (Managua: Academia nicaragüense de la lengua, 2011).

Darío, Rubén, *El mundo de los sueños*, ed. by Ángel Rama (Río Piedras: Editorial Universitaria, Universidad De Puerto Rico, 1973).

Darío, Rubén, *Escritos dispersos de Rubén Darío*, ed. by Pedro Luis Barcia, 2 vols (La Plata: Universidad Nacional de la Plata, 1968–77).

Darío, Rubén, *Escritos inéditos*, ed. by Erin K. Mapes (New York: Instituto de las Españas en los Estados Unidos, 1938).

Darío, Rubén, *Los Raros*, ed. by Günter Schmigalle (Berlin: Verlag Walter Frey, 2015).

Darío, Rubén, *Obras Completas*, 10 vols (Madrid: Mundo Latino, 1917).

Darío, Rubén, *Peregrinaciones* (Paris: Imprenta de la Vda de Ch. Bouret, 1901).

Darío, Rubén, *Poesía*, ed. by Ernesto Mejía Sánchez (Caracas: Biblioteca Ayacucho, 1977).

Darío, Rubén, *Quince prólogos de Rubén Darío* (Managua: Instituto nicaragüense de cultura, 1997).

De Castro, Eugénio, *Obras poéticas*, 10 vols (Lisboa: Imprensa Nacional, 1923).

De la Selva, Salomón, *Tropical Town and Other Poems* (Houston: Arte Público Press, 1997).

De la Selva, Salomón, *Versos y versiones nobles y sentimentales* (Managua: Banco de América, 1975).

De la Selva, Salomón and Thomas Walsh, *Eleven Poems* (New York: G.P. Putnam, 1916).

De Man, Paul, *The Rhetoric of Romanticism* (New York: Columbia University Press, 1984).

Del Greco, Arnold Armand, *Repertorio bibliográfico del mundo de Rubén Darío* (New York: Las Américas, 1969).

Delgado, Leonel, "La vida de Rubén Darío escrita por él mismo. Escritura autobiográfica y políticas del nombre," *Istmo*, vol. 10, enero–junio (2005). http://istmo.denison.edu/n10/articulos/vida.html#end3.

Demorizi, Emilio Rodríguez, ed., *Rubén Darío y sus amigos dominicanos* (Bogotá: Ediciones Espiral Colombia, 1948).

Derusha, Will and Alberto Acereda, *Songs of Life and Hope* (North Carolina: Duke University Press, 2004).

Díaz, Isabel, "Traducciones de la obra de Rubén Darío a la lengua inglesa," *Miradas críticas sobre Rubén Darío*, ed. by Nicasio Urbina (Managua: PAVSA, 2005): 281–92.

Díez-Canedo, Enrique, *Del cercado ajeno: versiones poéticas* (Madrid: M. Pérez Villavicencio, 1907).

Douglas Challener, Scott, *From the Outside: Latin American Anthologies and the Making of U.S. Literature*, October 2019, Rutgers University. PhD Dissertation. https://rucore.libraries.rutgers.edu/rutgers-lib/61706/PDF/1/play/.

Eliot, Thomas S., *The Sacred Wood: Essays on Poetry and Criticism* (London: Methuen, 1970).

Ellis, Keith, *Critical Approaches to Rubén Darío* (Toronto: Toronto University Press, 1974).

Feinsod, Harris, *The Poetry of the Americas* (Oxford: Oxford University Press, 2017).

Feinstein, Adam, *Pablo Neruda: A Passion for Life* (London: Bloomsbury, 2004).

Fiore, Dolores Ackel, *Rubén Darío in Search of Inspiration: Greco-Roman Mythology in His Stories and Poetry* (New York: Las Américas, 1963).

Forster, Leonard, *The Poet's Tongues: Multilingualism in Literature* (Cambridge: Cambridge University Press, 2009).

Fowler, Roger, *Linguistic Criticism* (Oxford: Oxford University Press, 1996).

France, Peter, *The Oxford Guide to Literature in English Translation* (Oxford: Oxford University Press, 2000).
Galvin, Rachel, "Poetic Innovation and Appropriative Translation in the Americas," *A Companion to Translation Studies*, ed. by Sandra Bermann and Catherine Porter (Oxford: Wiley Blackwell, 2014): 361–74.
García Morales, Alfonso, "Paralela/mente 'El reino interior' como la 'obra maestra' de Rubén Darío," *Anales de Literatura Española*, no. 28 (2016): 99–117.
García Morales, Alfonso, "¿Qué triunfo celebra Darío en su 'Marcha triunfal'?," *Zama*, Extraordinario: Homenaje a Rubén Darío (2016): 48–68.
García Morales, Alfonso, "Un Artículo Desconocido De Rubén Darío: «Mallarmé. Notas Para Un Ensayo Futuro»," *Anales De Literatura Hispanoamericana*, vol. 35 (2006): 31–54.
Garfield, Evelyn Picón and Iván A. Schulman, *Las entrañas del vacío: ensayos sobre la modernidad hispanoamericana* (Mexico: Ediciones Cuadernos Americanos, 1984).
González Echevarría, Roberto, "The Master of Modernismo," *The Nation*, January 25, 2006. https://www.thenation.com/article/master-modernismo/ [accessed June 31, 2019].
González-Rodas, Publio, "Rubén Darío y el Conde de Lautréamont," *Revista Iberoamericana*, vol. 37, no. 75 (1971): 375–89.
Grigsby, Carlos F., "*El fracaso de París*: Rubén Darío's Modernista Campaign in France," *MLR*, vol. 114, no. 4 (October 2019): 614–33.
Grigsby, Carlos F., "The Different Lives of Rubén Darío's *Los raros*," *Bulletin of Spanish Studies*, vol. 95, no. 6 (2018): 679–706.
Guillén, Claudio, *Entre lo uno y lo diverso* (Barcleona: Crítica, 1985).
Hays, Hoffman R., *12 Spanish American Poets* (New Haven: Yale University Press, 1943).
Henríquez Ureña, Max, *Breve historia del modernismo* (Mexicp: Fondo de Cultura Económica, 1954).
Henríquez Ureña, Pedro, *Literary Currents in Hispanic America* (Cambridge, MA: Harvard University Press, 1945).
Henríquez Ureña, Pedro, "Rubén Darío y el siglo XV," *Revue Hispanique*, vol. L (1920): 324–7.
Hollander, John, *Vision and Resonance: Two Senses of Poetic Form* (New Haven: Yale University Press, 1985).
Horen, Elizabeth, "Unrepentant Traveler, Accidental Diplomat, Triumphant Nobel: Gabriela Mistral in Wartime Brazil," *Anales de Literatura Chilena*, Año 16, número 24 (diciembre, 2015): 253–78.

Hughes, Langston, *Selected poems of Gabriela Mistral* (London: Indiana University Press, 1972).

Hugo, Victor, *La Légende des Siècles* (Oxford: Blackwell, 1957).

Hulme, Peter, *The Dinner at Gonfarone's: Salomón de La Selva and his pan-American Project in Nueva York, 1915–1919* (Liverpool: Liverpool University Press, 2019).

Infante, Ignacio, *After Translation: The Transfer and Circulation of Modern Poetics across the Atlantic* (New York: Fordham University Press, 2013).

Jensen, Theodore W., "El pitagorismo en Las fuerzas extrañas de Lugones," *Otros mundos otros fuegos: Fantasía y realismo mágico en Iberoamérica, Memoria del XVI Congreso Internacional de Literatura Iberoamericana*, ed. by Donald A. Yates (East Lansing: Michigan University Press, 1975): 299–307.

Jirón Terán, José, *Bibliografía general de Rubén Darío (julio 1883–enero 1967)* (Managua: Comisión Nacional del Centenario, 1967).

Jitrik, Noé, *Las contradicciones del modernismo* (Mexico: Colegio de México, 1978).

Jrade, Catherine, *Rubén Darío and the Romantic Search for Unity* (Texas: University of Texas Press, 1983).

Julián Pérez, Alberto, *La poética de Rubén Darío: crisis post-romántica y modelos literarios modernistas* (Barcelona: Orígenes, 1992).

Kellman, Steven, *The Translingual Imagination* (Lincoln: University of Nebraska Press, 2000).

Kemp, Lysander, *Selected Poems of Rubén Darío* (Texas: University of Texas Press, 1965).

Kermode, Frank, *Romantic Image* (London: Routledge, 2002).

Kirkpatrick, Gwen, "Forgiving Rubén Darío," *Review: Literature and Arts of the Americas*, vol. 51, no. 2 (2018): 180–7.

Klengel, Susanne, "Gabriela Mistral (1945)," *Nobelpreisträgerinnen: 14 Shriftstellerinnen im Porträt*, ed. by Claudia Olk and Susanne Zepp (Berlin: De Gruyter, 2019): 87–107.

Koch, Kenneth, *The Collected Poems* (New York: Knopf, 2018).

Latin Vulgate: Helping You Understand Difficult Verses. http://www.latinvulgate.com/ [accessed April 24, 2017].

Leavitt, Sturgis E., *Hispano-American Literature in the United States: A Bibliography of Translations and Criticism* (Stanford: Stanford University Press, 1932).

Leavitt, Sturgis E., "The Teaching of Spanish in the United States," *Hispania*, vol. 44, no. 4 (December 1961): 591–625.

Lee, Muna, "A Painful Example," *Poetry*, vol. 22, no. 3 (June 1923): 165–8.

Lefevere, André, *Translation, Rewriting, and the Manipulation of Literary Fame* (London: Routledge, 1992).

Litvak, Lily, *España 1900: modernismo, anarquismo y fin de siglo* (Barcelona: Antropos, 1990).

Lombroso, Cesare, *The Man of Genius* (London: W. Scott, 1896).

López Estrada, Francisco, *Rubén Darío y la edad media: una perspectiva poco conocida sobre la vida y obra del escritor* (Barcelona: Planeta, 1971).

Lorenz, Erika, *Bajo el divino imperio de la música* (Managua: Academia nicaragüense de la lengua, 1960).

Lugones, Leopoldo, *Rubén Darío* (Buenos Aires: Ediciones Selectas América, 1916).

Mallarmé, Stéphane, *Œuvres Complètes* (Paris: Gallimard, 1970).

Mapes, Erwin K., ed., *Escritos inéditos de Rubén Darío* (New York: Instituto de las Españas, 1938).

Mapes, Erwin K., *L'influence française dans l'œuvre de Rubén Darío* (Paris: H. Champion, 1925).

Marambio, Soledad, *Sujetos del deseo: una exploración sobre la traducción amateur en los años del Panamericanismo* (Berlin/Boston: De Gruyter, 2021).

Marasso, Arturo, *Rubén Darío y su creación poética* (Buenos Aires: Editorial Kapelusz, 1954).

Martí, José, *Obras Completas: Edición Crítica, vol. 13, 1881–1882* (La Habana: Centro de Estudios Martianos, 2010).

Martínez, José María, "Los raros: arquitectura(s), jerarquías y filiaciones," *Zama*, Extraordinario: Homenaje a Rubén Darío (2016): 69–91.

Martínez Rivas, Carlos, "Watteau y su siglo en Rubén Darío," *Cuadernos Hispanoamericanos*, no. 212 (1967): 445–53.

Marzán, Julio, *The Spanish American Roots of William Carlos Williams* (Austin: University of Texas Press, 1994).

Mayhew, Johnathan, *Apocryphal Lorca: Translation, Parody, Kitsch* (Chicago: Chicago University Press, 2009).

McElduff, Siobhán, *Roman Theories of Translation: Surpassing the Source* (London: Routlege, 2013).

McGuinness, Patrick, ed., *Symbolism, Decadence, and the Fin de Siècle: French and European Perspectives* (Exeter: University of Exeter Press, 2000).

McMichael, Charles, *Prosas profanas and Other poems* (New York: Nicholas L. Brown, 1922).

Mejía Sánchez, Ernesto, *Cuestiones rubendarianas* (Madrid: Ediciones de la Revista de Occidente, 1970).

Mejía Sánchez, Ernesto, ed., *Estudios sobre Rubén Darío* (Mexico: Fondo de Cultura Económica, 1968).

Mejías-López, Alejandro, *The Inverted Conquest: The Myth of Modernity and the Transatlantic Onset of Modernism* (Nashville: Vanderbilt University Press, 2009).

Molloy, Sylvia, "Ser/decir: tácticas de un autorretrato," *Essays on Hispanic Literature in Honor of Edmund King*, ed. by Sylvia Molloy and Luis Fernández Cifuentes (London: Tamesis Books, 1983): 187–99.

Molloy, Sylvia, "Voracidad y solipsismo en la poesía de Darío," *Zama*, Extraordinario: Homenaje a Rubén Darío (2016): 311–17.

Mordell, Albert, "Sketch of Hon. Charles B. McMichael," *Reminiscences and Essays*, ed. by Charles B. McMichael (Privately printed, 1922): 7–17.

Moréas, Jean, *Les Stances* (Paris: Mercure De France, 1929).

Moretti, Franco, *Distant Reading* (London: Verso, 2003).

Munday, Jeremy, *Stye and Ideology in Translation: Latin American Writing in English* (London: Routledge, 2007).

Navarro Tomás, Tomás, *Arte del verso* (Madrid: Visor, 2004).

Navarro Tomás, Tomás, *Los poetas en sus versos* (Barcelona: Ediciones Ariel, 1973).

Navarro Tomás, Tomás, *Métrica Española: Reseña Histórica y Descriptiva* (New York: Las Américas, 1966).

Neruda, Pablo, *Confieso que he vivido. Memorias* (Barcelona: Seix Barral, 1974).

Neruda, Pablo, *La Barcarola* (Buenos Aires: Losada, 1967).

Neruda, Pablo, *Twenty Love Poems and a Song of Despair*, trans. by William S. Merwin (New York: Penguin, 2003).

O'Conor-Bater, Kathleen Therese, *A Bilingual Anthology of Poems by Rubén Darío (1867–1916)* (New York: Edwin Mellen Press, 2015).

Ortega, Julio, *Rubén Darío* (Barcelona: Omega, 2003).

Pacheco, José Emilio, "Nota sobre la otra Vanguardia," *Revista Iberoamericana*, vol. 45, no. 106 (1979): 327–34.

Pacheco, José Emilio, "Prólogo 'Rubén Darío entre dos siglos,'" *Obras Completas I*, ed. by Rubén Darío (Barcelona: Galaxia Gutenberg, 2007): 27–47.

Paz, Octavio, *Cuadrivio: Darío, López Velarde, Pessoa, Cernuda* (Mexico: Joaquín Mortiz, 1965).

Paz, Octavio, *Los hijos del limo* (Barcelona: Seix Barral, 1974).

Pérez, Roberto Carlos, "Calderón de la Barca en Rubén Darío," *La Zebra*, no. 17 (May 1, 2017) https://lazebra.net/2017/05/01/roberto-carlos-perez-calderon-de-la-barca-en-ruben-dario-ensayo/ [accessed September 22, 2019].

Pérez Priego, Miguel Ángel, "'Dezires, layes y canciones' de Prosas profanas," *Anales de Literatura Española*, no. 28 (2016): 171–97.

Perus, Françoise, *Literatura y Sociedad en América Latina: el modernismo* (Havana: Casa de las Américas, 1976).

Piña-Rosales, Gerardo et al., eds., *Rubén Darío y los Estados Unidos* (New York: Academia Norteamericana de la Lengua Española, 2017).

Pittock, Murray, *Spectrum of Decadence: The Literature of the 1890s* (London: Routledge, 1993).

Pollack, Sarah, "Latin America Translated (Again): Roberto Bolaño's *The Savage Detectives* in the United States," *Comparative Literature*, vol. 61, no. 3 (2009): 346–65.

Pound, Ezra, *Literary Essays of Ezra Pound*, ed. by Thomas S. Eliot (London: Faber and Faber, 1954).

Pound, Ezra, *The Translations of Ezra Pound*, ed. by Hugh Kenner (New York: New Directions, 1953).

Prater, Donald, *A Ringing Glass: The Life of Rainer Maria Rilke* (Oxford: Oxford University Press, 1994).

Quevedo, Francisco de, *Poemas Escogidos* (Madrid: Castalia, 1989).

Quilis, Antonio, *Métrica española, edición actualizada y ampliada* (Madrid: Ariel, 1999).

Quintián, Andrés R., *Cultura y literatura españolas en Rubén Darío* (Madrid: Gredos, 1974).

Rama, Ángel, *Las máscaras democráticas del modernismo* (Montevideo: Arca Editorial, 1985).

Rama, Ángel, "Prólogo," *Poesía* (Caracas: Biblioteca Ayacucho, 1977): IX–LII.

Rama, Ángel, *Rubén Darío y el modernismo* (Caracas: Universidad Central de Venezuela, 1970).

Ramírez, Sergio, "El Libertador," *Del símbolo a la realidad: obra selecta de Rubén Darío* (Madrid: Alfaguara, 2016): XV–XLVI.

Ramos, Julio, *Desencuentros de la modernidad en América Latina: literatura y política en el siglo XIX* (Mexico: Fondo de Cultura Económica, 1989).

Rippy, J. Fred, "Literary Yankeephobia in Hispanic America," *The Journal of International Relations*, vol. 12, no. 3 (January 1922): 350–71.

Risco, Antonio, *El demiurgo y su mundo: Hacia un nuevo enfoque de la obra de Valle-Inclán* (Madrid: Gredos, 1997).

Rodó, José Enrique, *José Enrique Rodó: crítico literario*, ed. by Jorge Rufinelli (Alicante: Instituto de Cultura Juan Gil-Albert, 1995).

Roof, María, "Rubén Darío en inglés: la poesía," *Revista Casa de las Américas*, no. 282 (enero–marzo/2016): 10–33.

Rosetti, Dante Gabriel, *Poems* (London: Dent, 1961).

Rossich, Albert, "An Overview of Literary Multilingualism," *Comparative Critical Studies*, vol. 15, no. 1 (2018): 47–67.

Ruiz Casanova, José Francisco, "Arthur Rimbaud," *Diccionario histórico de la traducción en España*, ed. by Francisco Lafarga and Luis Pegenaute (Madrid: Gredos, 2009): 974–5.

Saavedra Molina, Julio, *Los hexámetros castellanos y en particular los de Rubén Darío* (Santiago: Prensas de la Universidad de Chile, 1935).

Salinas, Pedro, *La poesía de Rubén Darío: ensayo sobre el tema y los temas del poeta* (Buenos Aires: Losada, 1948).

Sanín Cano, Baldomero, *El Oficio de Lector* (Caracas: Biblioteca Ayacucho, 1978).

Santiago, Silviano, *The Space In-between: Essays on Latin American Culture* (North Carolina: Duke University Press, 2001).

Schanzer-Boris Gaidasz, George, "Rubén Darío, Traductor de Gorki," *Revista Iberoamericana*, vol. 33, no. 64 (1967): 315–31.

Schulman, Iván A., *Génesis del Modernismo: Martí, Nájera, Silva, Casal* (Mexico: Colegio de México, 1966).

Schulman, Iván A., "Modernismo, revolución y pitagorismo en Martí," *Casa de la Américas*, no. 73 (1972): 45–55.

Scott, Clive, *Literary Translation and the Rediscovery of Reading* (Cambridge: Cambridge University Press, 2012).

Scott, Clive, *Translating Baudelaire* (Exeter: University of Exeter Press, 2000).

Scott, Clive, *Vers Libre* (Oxford: Oxford University Press, 1990).

Sequeira, Diego Manuel, *Rubén Darío, criollo; o, raíz y médula de su creación poética* (Buenos Aires: Guillermo Kraft Ltda., 1945).

Sherry, Vincent, *Modernism and the Reinvention of Decadence* (Cambridge: Cambridge University Press, 2015).

Siskind, Mariano, *Cosmopolitan Desires: Global Modernity and World Literature in Latin America* (Illinois: Northwestern University Press, 2014).

Skyrme, Raymond, *Rubén Darío and the Pythagorean Tradition* (Gainesville: University Presses of Florida, 1975).

Stavans, Illan and Steven White et al., *Selected Writings of Rubén Darío* (London: Penguin, 2005).

Sucre, Guillermo, *La máscara, la transparencia: ensayos sobre poesía hispanoamericana* (Caracas: Monte Ávila, 1975).

Sux, Alejandro, "Rubén Darío visto por Alejandro Sux," *Revista Hispánica Moderna*, año 12, no. 3/4 (July–October 1946): 302–20.

Symons, Arthur, *The Symbolist Movement in Literature*, ed. with an introduction by Matthew Creasy (Manchester: Carcanet, 2014).

Taylor-Batt, Juliette, *Multilingualism in Modernist Fiction* (London: Palgrave MacMillan, 2013).

Teicher, Craig Morgan, *We Begin in Gladness: How Poets Progress* (Minneapolis: Graywolf Press, 2018).

Torres Bodet, Jaime, *Rubén Darío—Abismo y cima—* (Mexico: Fondo de Cultura Económica, 1966).

Torres-Rioseco, Arturo, *Rubén Darío: Casticismo y Americanismo* (Cambridge, MA: Harvard University Press, 1931).

Tünnermann Bernheim, Carlos, "'Canto a la Argentina y otros poemas' de Darío," *La Prensa*, December 7, 2015. http://www.laprensa.com.ni/2015/12/07/columna-del-dia/1949723-canto-a-la-argentina-y-otros-poemas-de-dario [accessed April 24, 2017].

Vallejo, César, *Los Heraldos Negros* (Madrid: Cátedra, 1998).

Vallejo, César, *Scales: Melographed*, trans. by Joseph Mulligan (Middletown: Wesleyan University Press, 2017).

Vallejo, César, *Spain, Take This Chalice from Me and Other Poems*, trans. by Margaret Sayers Peden (New York: Penguin, 2008).

Vallejo, César, *The Complete Poetry: A Bilingual Edition*, trans. by Clayton Eshelman and José R. Barcia (Berkeley: University of California Press, 2009).

Vallejo, César, *Trilce*, trans. by Valentino Gianuzzi and Michael Smith (Exeter: Shearsman Books, 2005).

Venuti, Lawrence, *The Translator's Invisibility: A History of Translation* (London: Routledge, 2008).

Verlaine, Paul, *Œuvres Poétiques Complètes* (Paris: Bibliothèque de la Pléiade, 1962).

Wales, Katie, *A Dictionary of Stylistics* (London: Longman, 1990).

Walkowitz, Rebecca L., *Born Translated: The Contemporary Novel in an Age of World Literature* (New York: Columbia University Press, 2015).

Walsh, Thomas, *Hispanic Anthology* (New York: G.P. Putnam's Sons, 1920).

Watts, Ian, *The Rise of the Novel: Studies in Defoe, Richardson and Fielding* (London: Pimlico, 2000).

Weir, David, *Decadence and the Making of Modernism* (Amherst: University of Massachusetts Press, 1995).

West, David and Anthony J. Woodman, eds., *Creative Imitation and Latin Literature* (Cambridge: Cambridge University Press, 1979).

White, Steven, "Salomón de la Selva: Testimonial Poetry and World War I," *Modern Nicaraguan Poetry: Dialogues with France and the United States* (London: Associated University Press, 1993): 119–43.

Williams, William Carlos, *By Word of Mouth: Poem from the Spanish, 1916–1959* (New York: New Directions, 2011).

Woodbridge, Hensley Charles, *Rubén Darío, a Selective Classified and Annotated Bibliography* (Metuchen, NJ: Scarecrow, 1975).

Woods, Michelle, *Kafka Translated* (New York: Bloomsbury Academic, 2013).

Yao, Steven G., *Translation and the Languages of Modernismo. Gender, Politics, and Language* (New York: Palgrave, 2003).

Yildiz, Yasemin, *Beyond the Mother Tongue: The Postmonolingual Condition* (New York: Fordham University Press, 2012).

Yurkiévich, Saúl, *Celebración del Modernismo* (Barcelona: Tusquets, 1976).

Zanetti, Susana, ed., *Las Cenizas de la Huella: linajes y figuras de artista en torno al modernismo* (Buenos Aires: Viterbo Editora, 1997).

Zavala, Iris, "Sobre la elaboración de 'Cosas del Cid' de Rubén Darío," *Hispanic Review*, vol. 47, no. 2 (1979): 125–47.

Zumthor, Paul, "Un problème d'esthétique médiévale: l'utilisation poétique du bilinguisme," *Le Moyen Age*, vol. XV (1960): 301–36; 561–94.

Index

AAUP (American Association of University Presses) 106
Acereda, Alberto 5, 109
Aira, César 108
Anacreon 53
Anderson Imbert, Enrique 7, 130
Appelbaum, Stanley 113–15, 118, 121, 128
Arielismo 75–6
Art nouveau 95
Attridge, Derek 29

Banville, Théodore de 29, 31–4, 37–8, 45, 53
Barbey d'Aurevilly, Jules 29
Baudelaire, Charles 44, 99, 126
Bellitt, Ben 102–3
Berceo, Gonzalo de 49, 51, 53
Blackwell, Alice Stone 14, 77, 80–4, 87–9, 121
Bly, Robert 86, 102, 104
Bolaño, Roberto 108
Boll, Tom 4
Book-length translations of Darío into English
    Eleven poems 79, 90, 100
    Rubén Darío: Selected Writings 16, 71, 108, 114–17, 119–20
    Selected Poems of Rubén Darío: A Bilingual Anthology 15, 108
    Songs of Life and Hope 15, 108, 118, 121, 123
    Stories and Poems/Cuentos y Poesías: A Dual-Language Book 15, 109
Borges, Jorge Luis 1–2, 5–6, 11, 83, 86, 91, 105, 107–10
Botticelli, Sandro 41
Bowra, Maurice 73–4, 98

Cardenal, Ernesto 4
Carrera Andrade, Jorge 84, 86
Cernuda, Luis 99
Cervantes, Miguel de 5, 54–5, 58
    Don Quijote 54–6

CIAR (Center of Inter-American Relations) 106
Coppée, François 13
Cosmopolita
    Cosmopolitan 10, 83
    Cosmopolitanism 30, 43, 66
    Movimiento cosmopolita 28
Cuban Revolution 73–4, 136

D'Annunzio, Gabriele 111, 137
Dante 40, 58
de Armas, Augusto 28, 45
de Castro, Eugénio 28, 39–44, 111
de la Selva, Salomón 14, 15, 75, 77–8, 80, 91, 100–2, 115–21
    El soldado desconocido 101
de Lisle, Leconte 31
de Onís, Harriet 73, 80, 88
Derusha, Will 5, 109
    and Alberto Acereda 91, 113
Dundas Craig, G. 83–4, 121

Eliot, T.S. 76, 88, 90, 92, 110
Eshleman, Clayton 102–3

Feinsod, Harris 80, 85
Fin-de-siécle 92–3, 97, 111
    literature 90
    poetics 107
    poetry 111
    poets 120, 136
Fitts, Dudley 85–7, 106

García Lorca, Federico 4, 5, 106, 109
García Márquez, Gabriel 72, 108
Gautier, Théophile 24, 29, 34, 45, 53
Georg, Stefan 111, 137
Goldberg, Isaac 73, 75, 80–1, 83, 88
Góngora, Luis de 48–9, 53–6, 68
González Echevarría, Roberto 71–2, 109, 114
Good Neighbor Policy 14, 80

Groussac, Paul 7, 12–13, 22, 24, 48
Guillén, Claudio 10

Hays, H.R. 14, 86–7, 90
Henríquez Ureña, Pedro 4, 7, 8, 49–50, 79, 101, 106
Hispanic Society of America 78–9
Horace 57, 88
Hugo, Victor 26, 31, 53, 60, 126
Huidobro, Vicente 4, 83, 86
Hulme, Peter 75, 78, 80, 85

Ibsen, Henrik 28
Individual Works by Darío
    A. de Gilbert 21, 44
    Azul ... 21–7, 31, 79, 93
    Canto a la Argentina y otros poemas 22, 64
    Cantos de vida y esperanza 8, 47–8, 51, 58–60, 64, 82, 115
    El canto errante 22, 47, 58, 63–4, 66, 79, 125–6
    El salmo de la pluma 26
    Historia de mis libros 24, 27, 32, 40, 56, 61
    Peregrinaciones 95
    Prosas profanas 7, 16, 31, 43, 47, 49, 50, 58, 64, 111, 125–33, 135–57

Jiménez, Juan Ramón 4
Joyce, James 92
Julián Pérez, Alberto 34–5

Kemp, Lysander 15, 107, 115, 117–18, 120
Koch, Kenneth 105

Languages
    Catalan 10, 12, 16, 47, 49, 63–6, 68, 135
    Early Modern Spanish 10, 12, 16, 49, 53, 55
    French 4–5, 10–1, 13, 16, 21–45, 47–51, 64, 135
    Latin 12, 16, 49, 57–60, 62, 66, 135
    Provençal 10, 12, 16, 68
Latin hexameters 47, 59, 61, 63–4, 68
Lautréamont 28, 45
Lee, Muna 77, 79–80, 109, 121
Lefevere, André 88

Literary Magazines
    Mundial 22
    Others 76
    Pan-American Poetry 76–7
    Poetry 76
Literary movements
    European Avant-garde 98, 101
    Futurism 97
    Imagism 102, 111
    Modernism 14, 15, 88–92, 98, 101–2, 118, 132, 136–7
    Modernismo 4, 6, 83, 90–2, 95, 99, 125–7, 135
    modernista 109, 114, 126, 135–6
    Modernists 121
    Parnasse 31, 34, 90–1, 93, 97
    Parnassian craftsmanship 95
    Parnassians 122
    Posmodernismo 84, 86, 101
    Posmodernista 2, 77, 87, 136
    Romantic poets 108
    Romanticism 90, 99
    Surrealism 86, 111
    Symbolism 28, 57, 86, 90, 93, 95
    Symbolisme 58, 91–5, 98
    Vanguardias 91, 101
    Vanguardismo 84
    Vanguardistas 136
Lugones, Leopoldo 40, 65, 76–7

Machado, Antonio 4
Mallarmé, Stéphane 44
Mallorca 63–6
Mapes, Erwin K. 8, 12, 29, 33–4
Marambio, Soledad 80, 84, 88
Marasso, Arturo 8, 29, 33–4, 41, 43, 54, 63
Marinetti, Tommaso 14, 96–7, 99
    Futurist Manifesto 96
Martí, José 4, 26, 28, 48
McMichael, Charles 79, 85
Mejía Sánchez, Ernesto 10, 24, 99
Merwin, W.S. 103–4
Mistral, Gabriela 4, 14, 77, 87–9, 106
Molloy, Sylvia 57
Moréas, Jean 45, 57–8, 92–3, 100
Multilingualism 10, 12, 26–8, 135
    Multilingual poetics 64, 67–8
Munday, Jeremy 73

Navarro Tomás, Tomás 3, 5, 26
Neruda, Pablo 4, 15, 84, 86, 102–4, 106, 109, 137
Nordau, Max 28

Oliver Belmás, Antonio 9
Ortega, Julio 28

Pacheco, José Emilio 101–2, 109, 114
Palma, Ricardo 7, 67
Pan-Americanism 14, 75–6, 79–80
    experiments 136
    Pan-Americanists 87
    translators 86
Pan-Hispanism 48, 57, 76
Pan-Latinism 47
    Pan-Latinist 51
Paz, Octavio 56, 85, 91, 107, 109, 126
Penguin 2, 4, 16, 71–2, 109–10, 114, 121
Pérez, Alberto Julián 34–5
Poe, Edgar Allan 28, 39–40, 79, 90
Poems
    "Ama tu ritmo" 16, 127–31
    "Canto de esperanza" 115–18
    "¡Torres De Dios!… " 115, 118
Post-Boom 106
Prosody 109, 114, 122, 128, 130–31
    Latin 62
    Spanish-language 107
Provençal poetry 47, 49–51

Quevedo, Francisco de 53, 68

Rama, Ángel 7–8
Reyes, Alfonso 79
Rilke, Rainer Maria 86

Rimbaud, Arthur 14, 96–9
Rodenbach, George 64
Rodin, Auguste 14, 95–9
Rodó, José Enrique 7, 24, 50, 75
Rosetti, Dante Gabriel 40–1
Rothenberg, Jerome 102

Salinas, Pedro 9
Santiago, Silviano 30–1, 44
Schmigalle, Günter 58
Silva Castro, Raúl 9
Siskind, Mariano 9, 22
St. Vincent Millay, Edna 77, 101

Teicher, Craig Morgan 29
The "Boom" 15, 72, 78, 88–9, 106–7, 123, 136
Torres-Rioseco, Arturo 8

Unamuno, Miguel de 24

Valera, Juan 21, 25, 48
Vallejo, César 4, 5, 15, 74, 86, 91, 102, 104, 106, 109
Velázquez, Diego 53–4
Venuti, Lawrence 72, 88, 112
Verlaine, Paul 29, 36–7, 39, 41–5, 51–3, 98, 111, 137
Virgil 57–8, 62, 65

Walsh, Thomas 15, 80, 100
Williams, William Carlos 76, 89
World Literature(s) 9–10, 13
Wright, James 102

Yeats, William Butler 92, 109, 114

www.ingramcontent.com/pod-product-compliance
Lightning Source LLC
Chambersburg PA
CBHW052048300426
44117CB00012B/2019